Introducing the

SONG
SHEET

Introducing the
SONG SHEET

A Collector's Guide
With Current Price List

by Helen Westin

Thomas Nelson, Inc., Publishers

Nashville   New York

Acknowledgements

The song sheets listed below are used by permission. All rights are reserved to owners of copyrights.

Used by permission of Shapiro, Bernstein & Co. Inc.: "Down on the Farm," "Seven or Eleven" or "My Dixie Pair o' Dice," "Rolling in His Little Rolling Chair," "Long Boy."

Used by permission of Sam Fox Publishing Co. Inc.: "Little Colonel," "College Yell," "Co-ed."

Used by permission of Forster Music Publishing, Inc.: "Calico Rag," "Pink Poodle One Step," "The Cloud Kisser Rag."

Continued on page 159

All rights reserved under International and Pan-American Conventions. Published by Thomas Nelson, Inc., Publishers, Nashville, Tennessee. Manufactured in the United States of America.
Design by Harold Leach

Library of Congress Cataloging in Publication Data

Westin, Helen.
  Introducing the song sheet.

  Bibliography: p.
    1. Songs, American—Collectors and collecting. 2. Music, Popular (Songs, etc.)—United States—Collectors and collecting. I. Title.
ML111.W4   769'.5   75-40331
ISBN 0-8407-4325-4

Preface

I have been firmly enfolded in the arms of the crazy world of *Collectomania* for the past 12 years and have consecutively succumbed to the lure of antique clocks, art glass, and sheet music.

Prior to my initiation into the *Old Rush*, my extracurricular energies were lovingly spent absorbing all phases of music appreciation, including composing —decomposing as a piano teacher of mine once said. Of course, this slanderous statement stemmed purely from jealously as any fool with a tin ear would heartily affirm.

Since I was reluctant to completely abandon one state of involvement for the other, the happy conclusion was the combining of the two. This resulted in the *Song Sheet Caper.* The sights and sounds of sheet music collecting have surpassed all expectations. It was, at the beginning, and still is, pure unadulterated fun.

My heartfelt gratitude is extended to those who helped me with the preparation of this book:

The staff members of the main Portland, Oregon, Public Library for continual assistance and advice while I was researching this book.

Jean Koch, for the availability of her collection and needed advice.

Lorelie Billings, for song sheets of the "silent era" and others.

Thurley Shields, who contributed in ways too numerous to mention and for the loan of several song sheets used in the book.

Finally, to my husband, Kermit, for washing the dishes.

To the many collectors who are familiar with the rudiments of song sheet collecting, may this book serve to renew your enthusiasm. To the uninitiated, my hope for you—an absorbing insight into the music that helped mold a great nation.

Tunefully Yours,

Helen Westin

Introduction

Do your eardrums vibrate with pleasure on hearing a piano raggin' out a Joplin tune?

Do you have an uncontrollable desire to frame a particularly attractive song sheet?

Do your eyes remain glued to the cover, completely fascinated by the artistry displayed thereon?

Are you astonished that such artistry remains, almost totally, without recognition—except for that of *Norman Rockwell?*

Are you cognizant of the role Tin Pan Alley has played, grinding out the grist for the mill of human emotions over a period of—roughly—fifty years?

Are you aware that every struggle, every achievement, be it political, sporting, geographical, or moral, has been eulogized by tunes emanating from the alley?

Do you wish to collect something exclusively *U. S. A.,* since it more nearly parallels your life?

If your reply is *amen* to any of these questions, the collecting of sheet music is *right up your Tin Pan Alley!*

Contents

Introducing the

SONG SHEET

CHAPTER 1

Tin Pan
Alley—
A Resumé

Because the majority of song sheets available to collectors was published after the 1880s, and except for Walt Disney, Shirley Temple, and World War II, little interest is shown later than the thirties, this book will deal primarily with the time period known to the music publishing business as the Tin Pan Alley era.

To the multitude of citizens who by vocation or choice, nearly a century ago, traversed the sidewalks of what is later known as Tin Pan Alley (Twenty-eighth street between Fifth and Broadway in New York City), what a cacophony of sound must have bombarded the eardrums. Imagine a variety of songs being played in dissimilar keys on out-of-tune pianos—simultaneously! It must indeed have sounded like the clangor of tin pans. (Monroe Rosenfeld is reputedly responsible for the title.) Thus Tin Pan Alley was born. Thus the golden age of the piano was born, and as the fledgling publishing companies emerged, the tune smith, musically uneducated in the majority of cases, came into being. Tin Pan Alley gained impetus with the American industrial revolution then in its infancy. The piano had finally arrived. In my opinion, it was, and still remains the greatest medium of musical expression with the exception of the human voice. A debate might be forthcoming from the guitar and organ cult of today. However, music is still written first for the piano. This speaks for itself.

Tin Pan Alley was an outlaw at its inception, primarily because of the fact that the copyright law was not enforced to any great degree. The American Society of Composers and Publishers (ASCAP) was not to be formed for another thirty years. The Alley was a fertile ground for plagiarism. Songs were sold for a pittance. The success from these same songs provided the finance needed, in many instances, to enlarge the hole-in-the-wall publishing companies on Twenty-eighth Street. Many of the publishers were songwriters. Unhappy at selling their songs, which ultimately became hits, for such a small fee, they became their own publishers.

Many sins have been attributed to Tin Pan Alley. How can we pass judgment on this giant—this giant that supplied the music that unlocked a nation's emotions and by giving vent to them, preserved, at least temporarily, its sanity.

Its life span was a mere fifty years. It is said that a star is brightest in its ascendency. So it was with Tin Pan Alley. So too, new stars are continually being born and their ascending brightness paling the others. The new stars, in this instance, were mechanical music (player piano, phonograph), radio, and motion pictures. The former two gradually sapped the Alley's strength, taking all and giving little in return. The great giant who wielded the final death blow was the movies. When sound became synchronized with film in 1926, the demand for music to lift the silents out of the doldrums was astronomical. To further this end, publishing companies were literally bought outright by the film tycoons and transplanted within the movie companies themselves. Tin Pan Alley was no longer its own master. It served new masters—the movie, record, and radio industries.

Obituary

Tin Pan Alley. Born sometime during the 1880s. Died in the 1930s. A lusty outlaw with a beautiful soul. May its offspring serve humanity as well.

CHAPTER 2

Do, Re, Mi's of Song Sheet Collecting

CATEGORIES— UNLIMITED!

efore settling down to categories, I would like to bring your attention to the following: You may have noticed that I have used, variously, two terms dealing with published music. These are *sheet music* and *song sheet*. Although sheet music is perfectly acceptable, it is a generic term, covering a broad field of published music, including classical, popular, instrumental, and voice editions. The term song sheet more nearly parallels the popular song concept of *words* and *music*.

There is not one doubt in my mind that *song sheets* provide a broader area of categories than any other field of collecting. Inside the covers lies the music of the Tin Pan Alley titans, plus that of a multitude of lesser tune smiths. The song sheet covers are a panoramic display of the country's character and history, drawn by artists heretofore relegated to the piano bench.

There are two distinctly different breeds of song sheet collector. The first collect for the music, the second, for the cover.

The music, of course, blankets a vast area. This includes composers, stage shows, theme music from the silents, Walt Disney, the various dances and rhythms, locations, communications, political, news songs, tear-jerkers, mother, and novelty songs. To collect by cover would encompass the cover artists (plus *Paull* lithographs and cartoonists), Art Deco, advertising song sheets, girl's portraits, clothing, action western, and other categories.

In addition to the thirty-eight categories represented in this book, one can include weather, money, occupations, college— you name it—it's all there in black and white piano music, wrapped in appropriate and colorful covers. There are dozens more. Like "The Little Old Clock on the Mantel" to a clock collector or "Red Wing" to an Indian collector, the song sheets also serve to enhance other collections. It is my intention to familiarize the reader with only basic categories. It would be virtually impossible to include them all in the confines of one volume.

Mention here should be made concerning tunes that fall into *multiple* categories. Take into consideration "When We Were

Two Little Boys." It tells the heart-breaking tale of two child-hood playmates, who were coincidently reunited during the course of a war, as one lay dying of battle wounds. This then can be placed in any of five categories—tear-jerker, children, war, cover artist, or composer.

Individual songs were often issued under several different covers, and the same cover design was frequently issued with separate performing artists.

MORTALITY RATE—HIGH!

The lamentable condition of any available song sheet is reason enough to preserve what is remaining in acceptable condition.

Why these wretched piles of torn, taped, dog-eared and smeared music with, by all means, the omnipresent owner's autograph in ink? They were played, thumbed, replayed, and literally torn to shreds while the song was in vogue, and then for sentimental reasons, or otherwise, stored in boxes or trunks to be rediscovered by a super-curious generation oriented to tape decks and transistor radios.

This same stack of old song sheets is not too interesting a sight. Included will be black and white issues published for music students, plus instrumental editions, voice, and special arrangements. These should be ignored. They should, however, not be confused with the black and white engravings and lithographs of the pre–1900 era. The majority of music published prior to 1900 had covers decorated with black and white engravings. To pass these up would be a mistake. A little experience will enable one to differentiate between the two. The pre–1900 black and white engravings consist of fine lines. The name of the engraving or lithograph company was ordinarily placed somewhere near the bottom of the song sheet—but look elsewhere.

There exist hundreds of sheet music collections in remarkably excellent condition. These were garnered at a much earlier time. We should be grateful for the interest that sparked these collections.

A sad commentary on song sheet collecting is the fact that the Tin Pan Alley classic song sheets so popular in their time and so desirable now as an addition to any collection were literally left in tatters by constant usage. As with any other collectible item, an unused or mint condition song sheet is an ultimate goal. But because of the reason stated here, we should perhaps be satisfied with a not-too-perfect example.

I have divided the song sheets' condition in order of their acceptability to a collection.

Condition	Value
Mint, near music store condition; absence of names, smears, tears or frays	100%
Music store stamp; otherwise mint	90%
Owner's name in ink; otherwise very good	75%
Carefully trimmed edges; otherwise very good	65%
Separated cover; otherwise very good	55%
Dog-eared or slightly frayed	50%
Torn, somewhat smeared, or badly frayed	25%
Dirty, badly torn, or incomplete	10%

DATING A SONG SHEET

There are two basic sheet music sizes to be concerned with. Prior to 1917, with rare exceptions, all music was published in the large (13½" × 10½") size. From 1920 onward all music was published in the standard (12" × 9") size. Dimensions in both instances vary as much as an inch. The transition period (1917 to 1919) was during the First World War. As in any great conflict, sacrifice of a nation's resources was prerequisite, and paper was no exception. These three years saw music published in four different sizes—large, standard, small, and miniature. The small (10" × 7") was intended to further the war effort. A miniature version (4" × 5") was distributed free to those in the armed services.

Concluding that all popular music was published in the standard size from 1920 on, it is easy to date a late or early issue of a particular piece of music by its size. This holds true provided the first release was prior to 1917. For example, the first issue of "In My Merry Oldsmobile" was in 1905—large sized. A revival of the song caused reissue after 1926 in the standard size.

"Now try this over on your piano" was a stock phrase used extensively to advertise the publisher's current song issues. They were printed on the back cover or on the inside of the front cover. These current song samples normally had their copyright dates listed just below a printed line of the song. *Now pay close attention.* If the copyright date of these current, advertised song samples was at a later date than the song's copyright on which advertised, one must conclude that the song in question was issued about the same time as the latest copyright date listed below the song samples. Therefore, it would not be the earliest issue.

A designated (first release) issue is unusual to find. If discovered, it certainly serves to simplify matters. "Miss Samantha Johnson's Wedding Day" (collection of the author) has this magic phrase on the front cover, thereby enhancing its value.

A copyright transfer is an additional clue. However, this must be coupled with research. So consult your public library's music department. There are many fine books on Tin Pan Alley (see Bibliography).

A fitting example of a copyright transfer is *William C. Handy's* "Memphis Blues." This song was first published by Handy, but the copyright was later transferred to *Theron C. Bennett* and subsequently to *Joe Morris Publishing Company.* W. C. Handy's original publication would be under the classification of Rare imprints. Look for these!

FIRST RELEASES

"You're a Grand Old Rag." Read it again. "Rag" is not a typographical error! The original title to George M. Cohan's famous song referred to our flag as a "rag." Publication was ceased almost immediately, and copies of the song hurriedly retrieved. It was reissued without delay in its present form, "You're a Grand Old Flag." The song's copyright date was 1906. This would most certainly be one of the rarest of imprints. Your chance of acquiring this gem—very remote.

It would serve us well if all initial song releases were designated *first release*. Seldom does one encounter this term, and as a consequence, we are forced to become tune detectives. First Release songs or imprints, like first edition books, are much sought after.

For whatever reason a copyright transfer was instituted, it is the one and only concrete clue to a first release. At the bottom of the title page (not the cover but the first page of song) is the copyright date of the song. This normally coincides with publication of the song. If the copyright has been transferred to another company, the original owner's date of copyright is listed first. Below this is the new owner of copyright and date.

Marches, intermezzos and waltzes, if successful, often prompted the publishing companies to call in a lyricist, thereby converting a popular vehicle into a singable ballad—recopyrighting it in this form. On occasion, the song was sold to another company, which in turn supplied lyrics and published it as a ballad. This called for a copyright transfer.

A songwriter would sometimes publish his own song. Perhaps he was unable to interest a publisher. Then again maybe he wished to reap all the profits. If his song attained any degree of acceptance by the public, publishing companies became eager for a copyright transfer. William C. Handy published his own "Memphis Blues" in 1912. Later Theron C. Bennett and Joe Morris became subsequent owners of the copyright. Much later another was issued by the Handy Brothers Publishing Company.

At the end of this chapter is a sample listing of songs having copyright transfers. Earliest and latest copyrights are given.

CAUTION, CARE, AND REPAIR

The first obvious pitfall to be on the alert for is an incomplete copy. At least half of all song sheets had an insert sheet. Check the pages to see if they are numbered consecutively. This may sound a bit elementary, but insert sheets are easily ignored.

One should not wholly disregard an incomplete song sheet any more than one would a complete edition of a torn, defaced,

---

* Martin, Deac: *Musical Americana.* (Englewood Cliffs, N.J.: Prentice-Hall, Inc., 1970.)

or dirty one. The insert sheet of a reject can be used in combination with an incomplete copy. These can be obtained at minimal cost.

"Horrified!" is the word to best express my reaction when offered my first *cut down* song sheet. There were at least forty very desirable rags for sale, and not less than twenty-five were on my Rags Wanted list—all cut down to fit a piano bench.

Prior to the twenties, nearly all pianos came with a stool. Sheet music cabinets were the proper place for sheet music. After the twenties, pianos came with benches formed to accommodate standard sized sheet music. If a new piano was purchased, what was done with the collection of large-size song sheets? The borders were whacked off with a scissors! The music was still intact, so who wanted to get up and trot over to the music cabinet for every selection when it was so easily available —right under your bottom?

It does not take an educated eye to spot a cut down song sheet. Little care was taken with regard to cutting off designs or portions of the lettering on the covers. They never seemed to be cut straight.

Trimmed edges are something else, again. A very narrow frayed edge is sometimes quite carefully scissored. To detect these, a trained eye is imperative.

Before filing, framing, or inserting in albums, go over your song sheet with a soft, dry cloth. The dirt removed in this manner will surprise you.

It is a mistake to attempt the removal of an ink signature by erasure or ink eradicator. A white area is the net result. Water colors may sometimes be used effectively to color the white worn or creased areas more noticeable on dark toned covers. A pencil signature is most often satisfactorily removed with a gum or rubber eraser. Care should be taken because too much pressure will eventually remove some of the color along with the signature.

Separated covers should be repaired in the following manner: Remove insert sheet. Place back and front covers so that spine edges are adjoining, and top and bottom edges are in a straight line (inner side of covers face up). Cut off about one-third inch transparent Scotch Tape* (I use a half inch width). Tack the two covers together with this small bit of tape, at approximately midpoint on the spine. This serves to keep the covers in position while you apply the final tape. Peel off a piece of tape one-half to one inch longer than the spine (this additional length makes it easier to start). The large-size sheet music would take a piece approximately 14½ to 15 inches in length. The standard size is 12½ to 13 inches. Starting with one fourth inch or more overlap (and be certain that cover edges touch), continue down entire spine. Cut off both top and bottom overlaps. Turn over song sheet covers (face side up). With a dry, clean soft cloth, move the hand firmly down length of spine. Fold together. Again, apply pressure along entire spine, causing it to lie flat. This does not detract in any manner from song sheet appearance. Badly frayed or torn edges should be repaired by taping along the inner edges of song sheet. This of course protects it from further damage in handling. Insert in albums; these may be purchased from certain stationary stores. Crown Albums of Los Angeles, no. B-480 fits large song sheets. Insert sheets may be added. As many as forty-eight song sheets can be inserted in one album.

LARGE VERSUS STANDARD SIZE SONG SHEETS

The difference in cover quality between the two sizes of song sheets is blatantly evident after one views thousands of each.

Why were the large size song sheets mainly more attractive than the standard size? This can be narrowed down to the reasons listed here.

1. The pre–1920 era artist used the entire color spectrum, having no decided preference for any particular color. Conversely, the 1920 to 1930 era seemed to be infatuated with the ubiquitous orange-blue, orange-green, orange-black, and orange-purple combinations.

2. As the movie and record industries blossomed, the preeminence of their stars became paramount, and as a result, singers

---

*Scotch "Majic Mend" or "Mystic" brand tape does not yellow or become brittle with age.

and movie stars became national idols. Their portraits were placed wherever they would gain the most exposure. In this respect the song sheets served the movie and record industry, and the decline in artistic covers commenced. This was true, to some extent, in the pre–1920 era to advertise Vaudeville, minstrels, and stage shows, but the trend became more common in the twenties, and by the thirties it was not usual to see a cover without a singing or movie star's portrait on the song sheet cover.

3. Simplicity of life in the thirties was reflected in an almost sterile quality in interior decoration. This was true on song sheet covers as well. An appropriate example is "While a Cigarette Was Burning." This song cover consists of a lone, lighted, glowing end of a cigarette. The remainder of cover is devoid of decoration.

To those whose interest lies in singing or movie stars, the twenties and thirties produced an unlimited supply.

Of course, the later the song sheet, the more selective one can be about condition.

OWN YOUR OWN GALLERY!

"Let's frame it!" These were the fatal words that resulted in the framing of "Red Wing." This ultimately led to my own gallery of Tin Pan Alley Classics, which number over a hundred.

The impact of an attractively framed song sheet is indescribable. It is almost akin to creating a work of art. A family room is the obvious place for display, but singularly or grouped, they will complement any room. What would be more appropriate than "Crabapple Rag" and "Candied Cherries Rag" for the kitchen or dining room? The decorating possibilities are endless.

It would be foolhardy to assume that an avid collector would have the facilities to accommodate the framing of an entire collection. Albums are available to protect song sheets. These albums consist of plastic envelopes sized perfectly to fit the music. The plastic envelopes, like the glass in the framing, transfigure mediocre appearing song sheets into attractive displays.

The phrase "I'm going to paper my party room with this old sheet music," leaves me horror stricken. The possibility of a cover being torn from a Joplin rag and smeared with wallpaper paste brings tears to my eyes. If you must wallpaper, use rejects. (Incidentally, this is an excellent idea.)

Framing is a personal expression. I prefer a narrow, white or black frame commonly found in variety stores. Sheet music has a tendency to be rather fussy, and ornate frames seem to add to the fussiness. I pin my songs on a burlap backing, leaving an appropriate matted border showing. I choose a predominant color used on the song sheet, matching it as closely as possible with the color of the burlap. I prefer framing song sheets in pairs. This takes some doing since the colors of the song sheets must be quite similar. Also the context should be of a like subject, I think. Matted to match, the result is very striking.

SONGS HAVING COPYRIGHT TRANSFERS

Any Old Port in a Storm	Maurice Richmond Inc.	1908
	M. Witmark & Sons	1908
At a Georgia Camptown Meeting (March-twostep)	Kerry Mills (F. A. Mills)	1897
	Kerry Mills	1899 (Song)
Canadian Capers	Roger Graham	1915
	Jerome Remick	1921
Castles in the Air	Appolo Verlog	1900
	Joe Stern	1900
Charmaine	Belwin, Inc.	1926
	Sherman Clay & Company	1927
Congratulations	Green and Stept Inc.	1929
	De Sylva, Brown & Henderson	1930
Go on, Good-a-Bye	Al W. Brown	1910
	Victor Kremer Company	1910
Hiawatha	Daniels & Russell	1901 (Piano)
	Whitney Warner Company (Assigned)	1902
	Whitney Warner Publishing Company	1903 (Song)

A Hot Time in the Old Town Tonight	Willis Woodward & Company	1896
	Theodore Metz (Renewed)	1924
	Ed B. Marks Company (Assigned)	1924
I Ain't Got Nobody	Craig & Company	1916
	Frank K. Root	1916
I'm Forever Blowing Bubbles	Kendis, Brackman Music Company	1919
	Jerome Remick & Company	1919
Kathleen	Helen Mora Corporation	1894
	Ed Marks Music	1930
Make Believe	Benny Davis Music Company	1921
	Waterson, Berlin Snyder	1921
Mary Lou	Henry Waterson, Inc.	1926
	Mills Music Company	1931
The Memphis Blues	W. C. Handy	1912
	Theron C. Bennett	1912
	Joe Morris Music	1916
Mickey	Daniels & Wilson Inc.	1918
	Waterson, Berlin, Snyder	1919
My Faithful Stradivarius	Joseph Weinberger	1912
	Joe Stern	1913
My Melancholy Baby	Joe Morris	1911
	Theron C. Bennett (Assigned)	1912
	Joe Morris Music (Assigned)	1912
My Pony Boy	The Date Music Company	1909
	Thomas J. Kennedy	1909
	Jerome H. Remick	1909
The Old Gray Mare	Panelle Music Company	1915
	Joe Morris Music	1917
The Preacher and the Bear	Eclipse Pub. Company	1904
	Joe Morris Company	1905
Red Wing	F. A. Mills Company	1907
	Paull-Pioneer	1917
Shimmy Shi She Wobble	Roger Graham	1916
	Joseph Stern	1917
	Ed Marks (Assigned)	1921

Silver Threads Among the Gold	C. W. Harris	1873
	H. P. Danks	1901
	H. R. Danks, A. V. Danks	1915
	G. L. Danks, L. V. Danks	
Smiles	Lee S. Roberts	1917
	Jerome R. Remick	1918
Song of the Islands	Bergstrom Music Company	1915
	Charles E. King	1917
That Naughty Waltz	Sol P. Levy	1919
	Forster Music Inc.	1920
They Didn't Believe Me	T. B. Harms	1914
	Joe Remick	1916
They Gotta Quit Kicking My Dog Around	Stark Music Company	1912
	M. Witmark & Sons	1912
Tumble Down Shack in Athlone	Oxford Music Pub. Company	1918
	Waterson, Berlin & Snyder	1918
Two Little Love Bees	Breitk Opf & Hortel	1909 (Leipsig)
	J. Stern & Company	1910
Whistling Rufus	F. A. Mills	1899 (Twostep)
		1899 (Song)

CHAPTER 3

The
Composers

**THE TIN PAN
ALLEY TITANS**

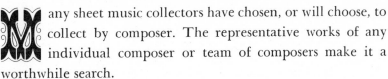 any sheet music collectors have chosen, or will choose, to collect by composer. The representative works of any individual composer or team of composers make it a worthwhile search.

It would be an endless task, serving no useful purpose, to delve even slightly into the lives of the Tin Pan Alley Titans. Their music speaks eloquently for them.

Although any change in musical taste is a gradual metamorphosis, there comes a time when old patterns are completely abandoned, never again to enjoy great popularity. By 1920 the public chose to be more honest about emotions. The overly sentimental, overly moral songs were not a true character reflection of the species *Homo sapiens*. In addition, the stigma attached to the Negro race was rapidly disappearing. *Coon* songs were no longer considered tasteful. The obsession for pathos was discarded. A new philosophy of life in general was apparent, and the outcrop of songs mirrored this.

With this philosophy in mind, my task would be much easier by dividing the composers into pre–1920 and post–1920 eras. But I have come to the conclusion that anything having to do with compiling information on song sheets is not a simple matter. How does one divide Irving Berlin? His popularity prior to 1920 was well established, and after 1920 his life was a saga of success. This was true to a degree of many individual songwriters or teams.

Like participants in a "tag waltz" (who nowadays ever heard of *that*?), changing partners was almost a way of life with words and music people. Eventually though a particular team of songwriters "clicked," and a more or less permanent partnership was the end result.

There were those who were perfectly capable of writing both words and music. Paul Dresser, George M. Cohan, James Thornton, Charles K. Harris, Irving Berlin, Walter Donaldson, and Cole Porter were completely self-sufficient. On occasion Irving Berlin collaborated with others. Walter Donaldson often worked with words people. He was equally successful by himself or teamed with a lyricist—in my opinion, a most undersung Tin Pan Alley man. Strictly a product of the post–1920 era, he also seemed to best capture this period in song. He is responsible, by himself or as the "music" man in a team, for an endless list of hits.

I am listing what I consider the major songwriters or teams from the early, middle, and late Tin Pan Alley eras. Listed separately, under sections entitled "Negro" and "Women' composers, are important writers belonging to these categories. If I am ever taken to task, it would most certainly have to do with the many composers I have excluded. See Chapter 4 for rag and march composers.

Early Tin Pan Alley	**Middle years**	**Late Tin Pan Alley**
Henry Dacre	Ernest R. Ball	Irving Berlin
Paul Dresser	Irving Berlin	Buddy De Sylva, Lew Brown,
Ed Harrigan and David	Will J. Cobb and	and Ray Henderson
Braham	Gus Edwards	Walter Donaldson
Charles K. Harris	George M. Cohan	Al Dubin and Harry Warren
Harry Kennedy	Raymond Egan and	Dorothy Fields and
Ed Marks and Joe Stern	Richard Whiting	Jimmy McHugh
Kerry (F. A.) Mills	Victor Herbert	Ira Gershwin and
Monroe Rosenfeld	Ballard MacDonald and	George Gershwin
William J. Scanlan	Harry Carroll	Jerome Kern
Joseph P. Skelly	Edward Madden and	Sam Lewis and Joe Young
Jim Thornton	Theodore Morse	Cole Porter
	Andrew Sterling and	Richard Rogers and
	Harry Von Tilzer	Lorenz Hart
	Albert Von Tilzer	
	Harry Williams and	
	Egbert Van Alstyne	

Early major songwriters (Song successes)

Harry Dacre

Daisy Bell (Bicycle Built For Two)   1892
Elsie From Chelsea   1896
Katie O'Conner   1891
Playmates   1889

Paul Dresser

The Blue and the Grey   1900
Calling to Her Boy Just Once Again   1900

Paul Dresser (cont'd)	The Convict and the Bird	1888
	The Curse of the Dreamer	1899
	I'ze Your Nigger If You Wants Me, Liza' Jane	1896
	Just Tell Them That You Saw Me	1895
	Mr. Volunteer, You Don't Belong to the Regulars	1901
	My Gal Sal	
	On the Banks of the Wabash Far Away	1899
	The Outcast Unknown	1887
	The Pardon Came Too Late	1891
	When You Come Back They'll Wonder Who the —— You Are	1902

Edward Harrigan and	Hats Off to Me	1890
David Braham	I've Come Here to Stay	1890
	Maggie Murphy's Home	1890
	My Dad's Dinner Pail	1883
	Paddy Duffy's Cart	1881
	Poverty's Tears Ebb and Flow	1885
	Taking in the Town	1890
	They Never Tell All What They Know	1893
	When the Clock in the Tower Strikes Twelve	1882

Charles K. Harris	After the Ball	1892
	Always in the Way	1903
	Better Than Gold	1895
	Break the News to Mother	1897
	Fallen By the Wayside	1892
	For Old Time's Sake	1900
	For Sale—a Baby	1903
	Hello Central, Give Me Heaven	1901
	In the City Where Nobody Cares	1910
	I've Just Come Back to Say Goodbye	1897
	'Mid the Green Fields of Virginia	1898
	There'll Come a Time	1895

Harry Kennedy	Cradle's Empty, Baby's Gone	1880
	Don't Forget the Old Folks at Home	1882
	I Had Fifteen Dollars in My Inside Pocket	1885
	I Owe Ten Dollars to O'Grady	1887
	Liberty (Written for Fund to Erect Satue of Liberty)	1884
	Little Empty Stockings	1883
	Molly and I and the Baby	1892
	Mrs. Brady's Daughter	1882
	Say Au Revoir But Not Goodbye	1893

Edward B. Marks and Joseph Stern	His Last Thoughts Were Of You
	The Little Lost Child 1896
	Mother Was a Lady (If Jack Were Only Here) 1896
	No One Ever Loved You More Than I

Kerry Mills (F. A. Mills)	At a Georgia Camptown Meeting 1897
	Happy Days in Dixie 1896
	Meet Me in St. Louis, Louis (with Andrew Sterling) 1904
	Rastus on Parade 1895
	Red Wing (with Thurland Chattaway) 1907
	Whistlin' Rufus 1899

Monroe Rosenfeld	Climbing Up the Golden Stairs (E. Heiser—pseudonym) 1884
	Gold Will Buy 'Most Anything But a True Girl's Heart 1898
	Her Golden Hair Was Hanging Down Her Back 1884
	Hush, Little Baby, Don't You Cry (F. Belasco) 1884
	I Don't Care If You Never Come Back 1897
	Johnny Get Your Gun 1886
	Just For the Sake of Our Daughter 1897
	Take Back Your Gold 1897
	Those Wedding Bells Shall Not Ring Out 1896
	With All Her Faults I Love Her Still 1888

William J. Scanlan	Gathering the Myrtle With May 1886
	If I Catch the Man That Taught Her to Dance 1882
	Moonlight at Killarney 1881
	My Maggie 1888
	My Nellie's Blue Eyes 1883
	Over the Mountain 1881
	Peek-A-Boo 1881
	Remember, Boy, You're Irish 1886
	There's Always a Seat in the Parlor For You 1881

Joseph P. Skelly	Are You Going to the Ball This Evening? 1881
	Behind the Parlor Door 1882
	The Finest on Parade 1883
	Little Darling, Dream of Me 1883
	Mother Is the Best Friend 1883
	My Pretty Red Rose 1877
	Strolling on the Brooklyn Bridge (With George Cooper) 1883
	Sweet Little Babies 1882
	A Violet I Picked From My Mother's Grave 1891
	Why Would We Meet as Strangers? 1891

James Thornton	Curious Cures 1897
	Don't Give Up the Old Love For the New 1896
	Going For a Pardon 1896
	It Don't Seem Like the Same Old Smile 1896
	My Sweetheart's the Man in the Moon 1892
	On the Benches in the Park 1896
	She May Have Seen Better Days 1894
	The Streets of Cairo 1893
	When I Took the Keeley Cure 1897
	When You Were Sweet Sixteen 1898

Songwriters of the Middle Years (Song successes)

Ernest R. Ball	All the World Will Be Jealous of Me (Words by Al Dubin) 1917
	Dear Little Boy of Mine (Words by J. Keirn Brennan) 1918
	Goodbye, Good Luck, God Bless You (Words by J. Keirn Brennan) 1916
	Let the Rest of the World Go By (Words by J. Keirn Brennan) 1919
	A Little Bit of Heaven, Sure They Called It Ireland (Words by J. Keirn Brennan) 1914
	Love Me and the World Is Mine (Words by David Reed, Jr.) 1906
	Till the Sands of the Desert Grow Cold (Words by George Graff) 1911
	Turn Back the Universe and Give Me Yesterday (Words by J. Keirn Brennan) 1916
	When Irish Eyes Are Smiling (Music with Chauncy Olcott; words by George Graff) 1912
	Will You Love Me in December as You Do in May 1905
Irving Berlin	Alexander's Ragtime Band 1911
	At the Devil's Ball 1912
	Everybody's Doin' It Now 1911
	He's a Rag Picker 1914
	Oh! How I Hate to Get Up in the Morning 1918
	Play a Simple Melody 1914
	A Pretty Girl is Like a Melody 1919
	Ragtime Violin 1911
	Say It With Music 1921
	That Mesmerizing Mendelssohn Tune 1909
	They Were All Out of Step But Jim 1918
	When That Midnight Choo-Choo Leaves Fro Alabam' 1913

Will D. Cobb and Gus Edwards*	By the Light of the Silv'ry Moon (Madden and Edwards) 1909
	Goodbye, Little Girl, Goodbye 1901
	I Can't Tell Why I Love Her But I Do 1900
	I Just Can't Make My Eyes Behave 1906
	If a Girl Like You Loved a Boy Like Me 1905
	If I Was a Millionaire 1910
	I'll Be With You When the Roses Bloom Again 1901
	In My Merry Oldsmobile (Bryan and Edwards) 1905
	In Zanzibar—My Little Chimpanzee 1904
	Mamie (Don't Feel Ashamee) 1901
	School Days 1907
	The Singer and the Song 1897
	Sunbonnet Sue 1906
	Tammany (Bryan and Edwards) 1905
	Waltz Me Around Again, Willie (Shields and Edwards) 1906
George M. Cohan	Forty-Five Minutes From Broadway 1905
	Give My Regards to Broadway 1904
	H-A-R-R-I-G-A-N 1907
	I Guess I'll Have to Telegraph My Baby 1898
	Mary's a Grand Old Name 1905
	Over There 1917
	So Long Mary 1905
	Under Any Old Flag at All 1907
	When a Fellow's on the Level With a Girl That's on the Square 1907
	When You Come Back 1918
	You're a Grand Old Flag 1906
Raymond Egan and Richard Whiting	I Wonder Where My Lovin' Man Has Gone (Words by Earle C. Jones; music by Whiting) 1914
	It's Tulip Time in Holland (Words by Dave Bradford) 1914
	The Japanese Sandman 1918
	Mammy's Little Coal Black Rose 1916
	Till We Meet Again 1918
	Ukelele Lady (Words by Gus Kahn) 1925
	When Shall We Meet Again 1925
	Where the Blackeyed Susans Grow 1917
	Where the Morning Glories Grow 1917
Victor Herbert	Absinthe Frappe (Words by Glen MacDonough) 1904
	Ah! Sweet Mystery of Life 1910
	Everyday Is Ladies Day to Me (Words by Henry Blossom) 1906

---

* All with Cobb as lyricist except where shown.

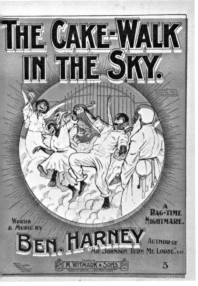

1899

2. 1897

3. 1914

1907

Figures 1 and 2. Examples of early cakewalks (Chapter 4).

Figures 3 and 4. "Those heavenly rags" (Chapter 4).

Figure 5. A fox trot (Chapter 4).

Figure 6. The popular "Rube" (farmer) character is featured here (Chapter 4).

Figures 7 and 8. Hesitations (Chapter 4).

5. 1914

7. 1916

8. 1914

1.   1914

2.   1915

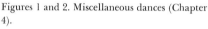

3.   1

4.   1907

Figures 1 and 2. Miscellaneous dances (Chapter 4).
Figure 3. Indian "Intermezzo" (Chapter 4).
Figure 4. Large size song sheet of "Red Wing" (Chapter 4).
Figures 5 and 6. Marches (Chapter 4).
Figure 7. A blues' song sheet (Chapter 4).
Figure 8. This song was introduced by the Duncan Sisters in "Tip Top" (Chapter 4).

5.   19

6.   1905

7.   1914

8.   19

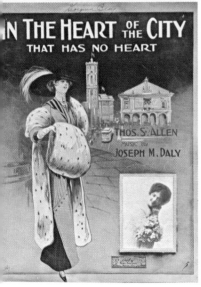

1913

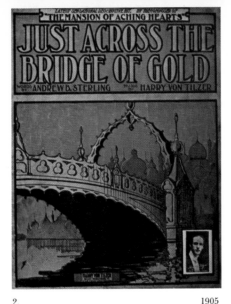

2.   1905

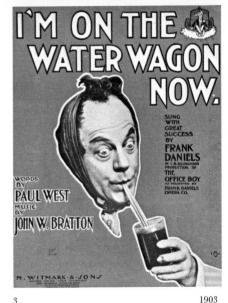

3.   1903

1910

Figures 1 and 2. Tear-jerkers (Chapter 5).
Figures 3 and 4. Songs about alcohol (Chapter 5).
Figure 5. A food song (Chapter 5).
Figure 6. An "Italian Immigrant" food song (Chapter 5).
Figures 7 and 8. Wearing apparel for both men and women (Chapter 5).

5.   1906

1910

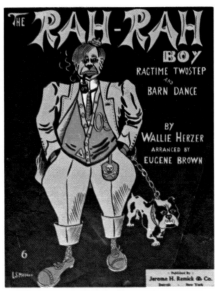

7.   1908

8.   1908

1.   1903

2.   1916

3.   19

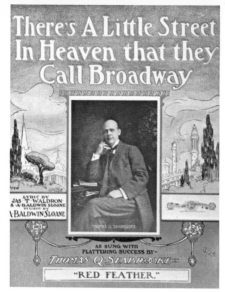

4.   1910

Figures 1 to 3. Songs about locations (Chapter 5).
Figure 4. Then as now, Reno was the place to get a quick divorce (Chapter 5).
Figure 5. A maudlin "mother" song (Chapter 5).
Figure 6. The cover of this "mother" song features Vitagraph star Jane Jennings (Chapter 5).
Figures 7 and 8. "Coon" songs (Chapter 5).

5.   18

6.   1918

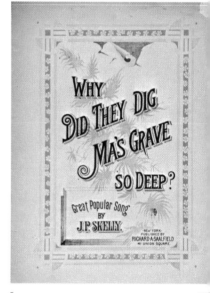

7.   1914

8.   19

1925

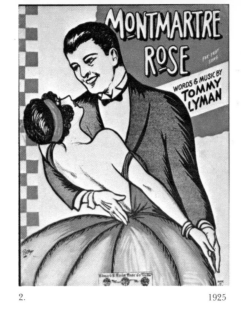

2.   1925

3.   1925

1925

Figures 1 and 2. Examples of girls' names and portraits (Chapter 5).

Figure 3. Cover by Saul Wohlman (Chapter 5).

Figure 4. Another song with a girl's name (Chapter 5).

Figures 5 and 6. Early automobile songs (Chapter 5).

Figure 7. Transportation song (Chapter 5).

Figure 8. Standard size song sheet of "In My Merry Oldsmobile" (Chapter 5).

5.   1909

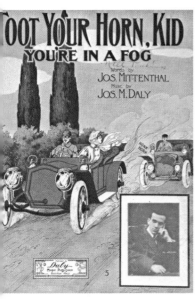

1909

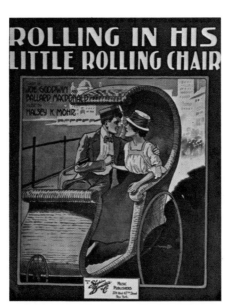

7.   1909

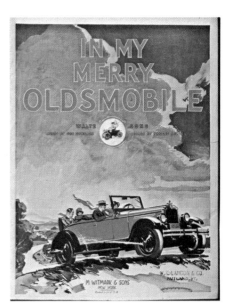

8.   1906

1.   1914

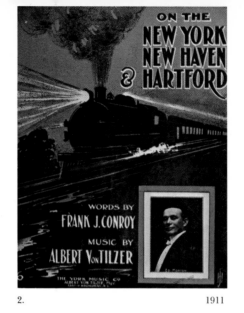

2.   1911

3.   19

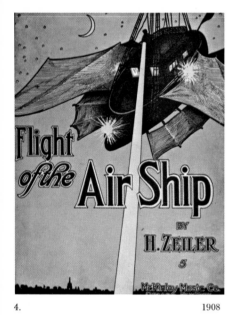

4.   1908

Figures 1 and 2. Songs about transportation (Chapter 5).

Figure 3. The glider was popular then (Chapter 5).

Figure 4. An early 1900 conception of a "UFO" (Chapter 5).

Figures 5 and 6. Songs showing forms of communication during the early years of the twentieth century (Chapter 5).

Figure 7. *The* most famous telephone song (Chapter 5).

Figure 8. Another communication song (Chapter 5).

5.   19

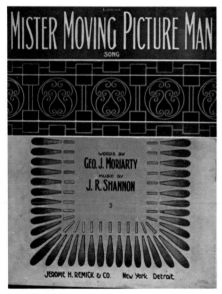

6.   1912

7.   1901

8.   19

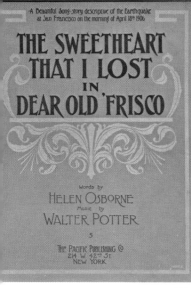

1906

2.   1933

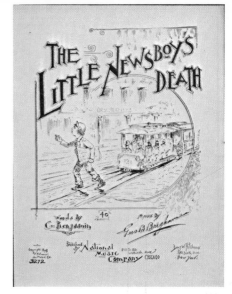

3.   1893

1915

Figure 1. A catastrophe song about the 1906 earthquake (Chapter 5).

Figure 2. A political song of the Depression era. Note N. R. A. symbol (Chapter 5).

Figure 3. This song was based on a news event.

Figure 4. The song was dedicated to Woodrow Wilson (Chapter 5).

Figure 5. This was written for the exposition (Chapter 5).

Figure 6. Written for the Portland, Oregon Rose Festival (Chapter 5).

Figure 7. This was dedicated to Ruth Chatterton (Chapter 5).

Figure 8. Dedicated to Abe Lyman by Charlie Chaplin (Chapter 5).

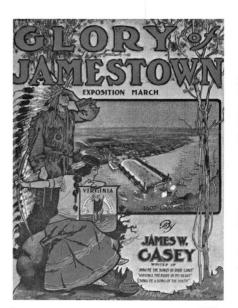

5.   1907

1909

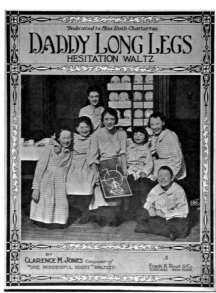

7.   1914

8.   1924

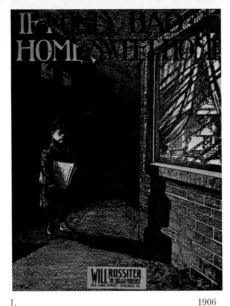

1.   1906

2.   1903

3.

4.   1910

Figures 1 and 2. Tear-jerkers about children (Chapter 5).

Figure 3. All Mammy's children were named after American generals of World War I (Chapter 5).

Figure 4. A "Mammy" croon (Chapter 5).

Figures 5 to 8. Songs about flora, fauna, and other earth creatures (Chapter 5).

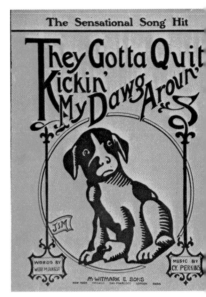

5.   1

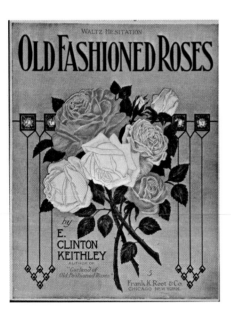

6.   1914

7.   1906

8.

1923

2.   1930

3.   1915

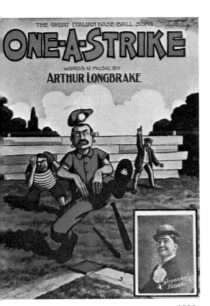

1908

Figures 1 and 2. Novelty songs (Chapter 5).
Figures 3 and 4. Songs about sports (Chapter 5).
Figures 5 and 6. Songs featuring games (Chapter 5).
Figure 7. A conflict song (Chapter 5).
Figure 8. Gladys Leslie, a Vitagraph star, is shown on this cover.

5.   1920

1916

7.   1915

8.

1. 1897

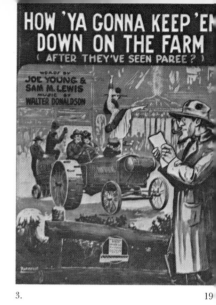

3. 19

4. 1919

Figure 1. A "mother" song (Chapter 5).

Figure 2. A popular war ballad of the day (Chapter 5).

Figure 3. This song was written just after the end of World War I (Chapter 5).

Figure 4. A World War I song (Chapter 5).

Figures 5 and 6. Early and late Starmer covers (Chapter 6).

Figure 7. The standard size reissue with the cover by Albert Barbelle (Chapter 6).

Figure 8. Andre DeTakacs is the cover artist (Chapter 6).

5. 190

6. 1919

7. 1907

8.

1915

2.   1918

3.   1920

1916

Figure 1. Pfeiffer is the cover artist (Chapter 6).
Figure 2. A John Frew cover (Chapter 6).
Figure 3. A Manning portrait (Chapter 6).
Figure 4. The initials R. S. are seen on the cover (Chapter 6).
Figure 5. Hap Hadley is the cover artist (Chapter 6).
Figure 6. An unsigned cover (Chapter 6).
Figure 7. Politzer is the cover artist (Chapter 6).
Figure 8. Cover by Leff (Chapter 6).

5.   1925

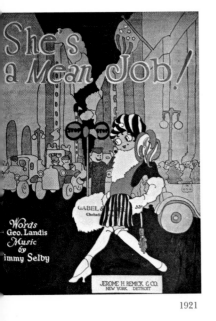

1921

7.   1923

8.   1925

1.   1920

2.   1921

3.   1[

4.   1912

Figure 1. Cover by Wohlman (Chapter 6).
Figure 2. Cover by P. M. Griffith (Chapter 6).
Figures 3 and 4. Unsigned covers (Chapter 6).
Figures 5 and 6. E. T. Paull Lithographs (Chapter 7).
Figure 7. Art Deco cover by Millard (Chapter 7).
Figure 8. Art Deco cover by Starmer (Chapter 7).

5.   19

6.   1905

7.   1920

8.   19

1904

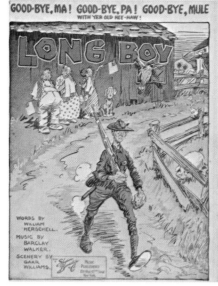

2. 1917

3. 1917

Figure 1. Cartoon cover by Swinnerton (Chapter 7).
Figure 2. Cartoon cover by Gaar Williams (Chapter 7).
Figure 3. Cartoon cover by De Beck (Chapter 7).
Figure 4. Cover by Carrie Jacobs-Bond, reproduced through permission of the copyright owners, Boston Music Co., 116 Boylston St., Boston, Mass. 02116.
Figure 5. Sunday Supplement cover (Chapter 7).
Figure 6. Action Western (Chapter 7).
Figures 7 and 8. Advertising song sheet, front and reverse (Chapter 7).

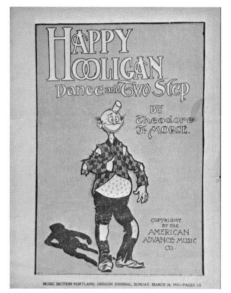

5. 1907

1911

7. Before 1920

8.

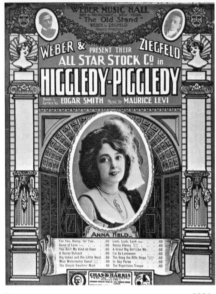

1.   1904

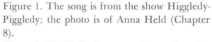

2.   1911

3.   1

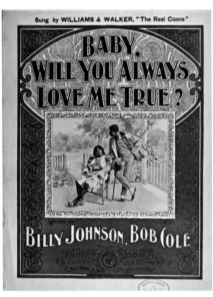

4.   1897

Figure 1. The song is from the show Higgledy-Piggledy; the photo is of Anna Held (Chapter 8).

Figure 2. The Dolly Sisters are featured on this cover of a song from the Ziegfeld Follies (Chapter 8).

Figure 3. Flo Irwin is the star on this cover (Chapter 8).

Figure 4. The team of Williams and Walker is shown here (Chapter 8).

Figure 5. From the "silent" movie *Heart's Ease* (Chapter 8).

Figure 6. This theme song was written at the end of the silent era (Chapter 8).

Figure 7. Pearl White, the star of *Perils of Pauline* is featured on this cover.

Figure 8. Francis X. Bushman, the pin-up boy of the silents, is shown here.

5.   1

6.   1929

7.   1914

8.

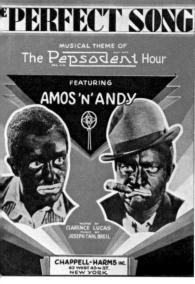

1915

2.   1923

3.   1948

1935

Figure 1. Radio stars Amos 'n Andy (Chapter 8).

Figure 2. This cover features Sophie Tucker (Chapter 8).

Figure 3. Song from Walt Disney's *Cinderella*, © Walt Disney Productions (Chapter 8).

Figure 4. Shirley Temple cover, reproduced by permission of Movietone Music Corp.—Sam Fox Publishing Co. sole agent (Chapter 9).

Figure 5. Art Deco cover.

Figure 6. The first Ragtime Waltz, by Harry Guy.

Figures 7 and 8. College Songs, reproduced by permission of Movietone Music Corp.—Sam Fox Publishing Co. sole agent.

5.   1913

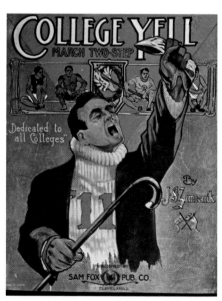

7.   1908

8.   1914

1.   1904

2.   1903

3.   19

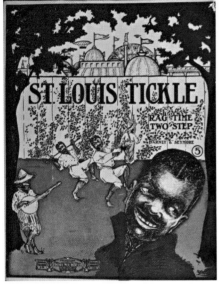

Figures 1 and 2. Two examples of songs written for the St. Louis World's Fair.

Figure 3. A song sheet from the Famous Dancer's Collection series.

Figure 4. Cover by Archie Gunn.

Figure 5. This cover features King Baggot, a silent film great.

Figure 6. A World War I special "peace" edition by Carrie Jacobs-Bond, reproduced by permission of the copyright owners, Boston Music Co., 116 Boylston St., Boston, Mass. 02116.

Figure 7. Other collectibles appear on song sheets.

Figure 8. One of the many dances popular at the time.

4.   5.   1

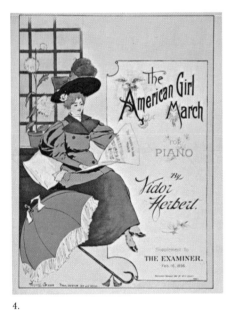

6.   1918

7.   1909

8.   1

Victor Herbert (cont'd)

Gypsy Love Song (Words by Harry B. Smith)   1898
I'm Falling in Love With Someone   1910
Italian Street Song   1910
A Kiss in the Dark (Words by Buddy De Sylva)   1922
The March of the Toys   1903
Sweethearts (Words by Harry B. Smith)   1913
Thine Alone (Words by Henry Blossom)   1917
Toyland (Words by Glen MacDonough)   1903
A Woman Is Only a Woman, But a Good Cigar Is a Smoke (Words
    by Harry B. Smith)   1905

Ballard MacDonald and
Harry Carrol

Beautiful Ohio (Words by Mary Earl [King]; music by Carrol)
    1918
Down in Bom-Bombay   1915
It Takes a Little Rain With the Sunshine to Make the World Go
    Round   1913
I've Got the Time, I've Got the Place, But It's Hard to Find the
    Girl (Words by S. Henry; music by Carrol)   1910
The Land of My Best Girl   1914
On the Mississippi   1912
Rose of Washington Square (Words by James F. Hanley; music by
    Carrol)   1917
She is the Sunshine of Virginia   1916
There's a Girl in the Heart of Maryland   1913
Tip Top Tipperary Mary   1915
The Trail of the Lonesome Pine   1913

Edward Madden and
Theodore F. Morse

Blue Bell   1904
Down in Jungle Town   1908
I Got a Feelin' For You; Way Down in My Heart   1904
I'd Rather Be a Lobster Than a Wise Guy   1908
The Lanky, Yankee Boys in Blue   1908
A Little Boy Called Taps   1904
Moonlight Bay (Madden and Wenrich)   1912
Nan! Nan! Nan!   1904
Please Come and Play in My Yard   1904
Two Blue Eyes   1907
Two Little Baby Shoes   1908
When You Wore a Pinafore   1908

Andrew Sterling and
Harry Von Tilzer

Alexander Don't You Love Your Baby No More   1904
Down Where the Cotton Blossoms Grow   1901
Hannah Won't You Open Up That Door   1904
I Wonder if She's Waiting   1899

Andrew Sterling and *Harry Von Tilzer* *(cont'd)*	My Old New Hampshire Home 1898 Wait 'Til the Sun Shines Nellie 1905 What You Goin' to Do When the Rent Comes Round? 1905 Where the Morning Glories Twine Around the Door 1904
Harry Von Tilzer and *Other Lyricists*	A Bird in a Gilded Cage (With Arthur Lamb) 1900 The Cubanola Glide (With Vincent Bryan) 1909 Down Where the Werzburger Flows (With Raymond Brown) 1902 The Mansion of Aching Hearts (With Arthur Lamb) 1902 On the Old Fall River Line (With Andrew Sterling and William Jerome) 1913 Under the Yum Yum Tree (With Andrew Sterling) 1910
Albert Von Tilzer	Give Me the Moonlight, Give Me the Girl (Words by Lew Brown) 1917 I'll Be With You in Apple Blossom Time 1920 The Moon Has Its Eyes on You (Words by Billy Johnson) 1905 Please Don't Take My Lovin' Man Away 1912 Pretty Baby (Words by Gus Kahn; music with Tony Jackson) 1916 Take Me Out to the Ball Game (Words by Jack Norworth) 1908 Teasing (Cecil Mack) 1904 That Old Girl of Mine (Words by Earle C. Jones) 1912 Wait Till You Get Them Up in the Air Boys (Words by Lew Brown) 1919
Harry Williams and *Egbert Van Alstyne*	Back, Back, Back to Baltimore 1904 Cheyenne 1906 Goodnight Ladies 1911 I'm Afraid to Come Home in the Dark 1907 In the Shade of the Old Apple Tree 1905 It Looks Like a Big Night Tonight 1908 Navajo 1903 Memories (Words by Gus Kahn; music by Van Alstyne) 1915 San Antonio 1907 There Never Was a Girl Like You 1906 What's the Matter With Father? 1910 Won't You Come Over to My House 1905

Major Songwriters of Late Tin Pan Alley (Song successes)

Irving Berlin	All Alone 1925 Blue Skies 1927 Cheek to Cheek 1935 Easter Parade 1933

Irving Berlin (cont'd)	God Bless America 1939
	How Deep Is the Ocean 1932
	Let's Face the Music and Dance 1936
	Remember 1925
	Russian Lullaby 1927
	Top Hat, White Tie and Tails 1935
Howard Deitz and Arthur Schwartz	Alone Together 1932
	Dancing in the Dark 1931
	I Love Louisa 1931
	If There Is Someone Lovelier Than You 1934
	Louisiana Hayride 1932
	Love Is a Dancing Thing 1935
	New Sun in the Sky 1931
	A Shine on Your Shoes 1932
	Something to Remember You By 1930
	You and the Night and the Music 1934
De Sylva, Brown, and Henderson	Aren't We All 1929
	The Best Things in Life Are Free 1927
	The Birth of the Blues 1926
	Black Bottom 1926
	Button Up Your Overcoat 1928
	If I Had a Talking Picture of You 1929
	It All Depends on You 1926
	Just a Memory 1927
	Keep Your Sunny Side Up 1929
	Life is Just a Bowl of Cherries (Brown and Henderson) 1931
	The Varsity Drag 1927
	You're the Cream in My Coffee 1928
*Walter Donaldson**	At Sundown 1927
	Carolina in the Morning (Words by Gus Kahn) 1922
	Georgia (Words by Howard Johnson) 1922
	How Ya Gonna Keep 'em Down on the Farm? (Words by Lewis and Young) 1919
	Kansas City, Kitty (Words by Edgar Leslie) 1929
	Little White Lies 1930
	Love Me or Leave Me (Words by Gus Kahn) 1928
	Makin' Whoopee (Words by Gus Kahn) 1928
	My Blue Heaven (Words by George Whiting) 1927
	My Buddy (Words by Gus Kahn) 1922
	My Mammy (Words by Lewis and Young) 1929
	That Certain Party (Words by Gus Kahn) 1925
	Yes Sir, That's My Baby (Words by Gus Kahn) 1925

*Alone or with others.

Al Dubin and *Harry Warren*	About a Quarter to Nine 1935 The Boulevard of Broken Dreams 1933 The Gold Diggers' Song (We're in the Money) 1933 I Only Have Eyes For You 1934 I'll String Along With You 1934 September in the Rain 1937 Shadow Waltz 1933 Shuffle Off to Buffalo 1932 Where Am I 1935 Wonder Bar 1934
Dorothy Fields and *Jimmy McHugh*	Cuban Love Song (With Herbert Stolhart) 1931 Diga, Diga Doo 1928 Don't Blame Me 1932 Exactly Like You 1930 I Can't Give You Anything But Love, Baby 1928 I Feel a Song Coming On 1935 I'm in the Mood For Love 1935 Lost in a Fog 1934 On the Sunny Side of the Street 1930 Thank You For a Lovely Evening 1934

Ira Gershwin and
George Gershwin
	Bess, You Is My Woman (Words by Ira Gershwin and Dubose
	    Heyward) 1935
	Bidin' My Time 1930
	Clap Yo' Hands 1926
	I Got Plenty O' Nuttin' (Words by Ira Gershwin and Dubose
	    Heyward) 1935
	I Got Rhythm 1930
	It Ain't Necessarily So 1935
	Of Thee I Sing 1931
	Someone to Watch Over Me 1926
	Strike Up the Band 1927
	Summertime 1935
	'Swonderful 1927

Jerome Kern	Bill (Words by P. G. Wodehouse and Oscar Hammerstein II)
	    1927
	Can't Help Lovin' Dat Man (Words by P. J. Wodehouse and Oscar
	    Hammerstein II) 1927
	I've Told Every Little Star (Words by Oscar Hammerstein II)
	    1932
	Look For the Silver Lining (Words by Bud De Sylva) 1920
	Make Believe (Words by Oscar Hammerstein II) 1927
	The Night Was Made for Love (Words by Otto Harbach) 1931

Jerome Kern (cont'd)	Ol' Man River (Words by Oscar Hammerstein II)	1927
	Smoke Gets in Your Eyes (Words by Otto Harbach)	1933
	They Didn't Believe Me (Words by Herbert Reynolds)	1914
	The Touch of Your Hand (Words by Otto Harbach)	1933
	Why Do I Love You (Words by Oscar Hammerstein II)	1927
	Why Was I Born? (Words by Oscar Hammerstein II)	1929

Sam M. Lewis and Joe Young	Cryin' For the Carolines (Music by Harry Warren)	1930
	Dinah 1925	
	Five Foot Two, Eyes of Blue 1925	
	Happy Go Lucky Land (Music by Joe Meyer) 1928	
	I'm Sitting on Top of the World 1925	
	In a Little Spanish Town (Music by Mabel Wayne) 1926	
	Keep Sweeping the Cobwebs off the Moon 1927	
	Laugh, Clown, Laugh (Music by Ted Fiorito) 1928	

Cole Porter	Anything Goes 1934
	Begin the Beguine 1935
	Blow, Gabriel, Blow 1934
	I Get a Kick Out of You 1934
	It's D'Lovely 1936
	I've Got You Under My Skin 1936
	Just One of Those Things 1935
	Let's Do It 1928
	Love for Sale 1930
	Night and Day 1932
	What Is This Thing Called Love? 1929
	You Do Something to Me 1929

Richard Rodgers and Lorenz Hart	Blue Moon 1934
	The Blue Room 1926
	Dancing on the Ceiling 1930
	Lover 1933
	Mimi 1932
	Mountain Greenery 1926
	My Heart Stood Still 1927
	My Romance 1935
	There's a Small Hotel 1936
	Thou Swell 1927
	With a Song in My Heart 1929
	You Took Advantage of Me 1928

Richard Whiting*	Ain't We Got Fun (Music by Ange Lorenzo and Richard Whiting) 1922

---

* See the middle years with Richard Egan.

Richard Whiting (cont'd)   Beyond the Blue Horizon (Words by Leo Robin; music with
                              W. Frank Harling)   1930
                              Breezin' Along With the Breeze   1926
                              Horses (Words by Byron Gay)   1926
                              Louise (Words by Leo Robin)   1929
                              My Future Just Passed (Words by George Marion, Jr.)   1930
                              On the Good Ship Lollipop (Sydney Clare)   1934
                              She's Funny That Way (Music by Neil Moret)   1928
                              Sleepy Time Gal (Words by Joseph Alden and Raymond Egan;
                              music with Lorenzo)   1925
                              True Blue Lou (Words by Sam Coslow and Lee Robin)   1929

NEGRO COMPOSERS

Soul—a wonderfully expressive but currently overused word, whose ancestry had little kinship with its modern counterpart. Had it occurred to anyone seventy or eighty years ago, it would have been just as applicable as it is now in describing the character essence of the Black person. One of the first professions open to the Negro race was that of music.

I may be stepping on toes, but in my estimation "Carry Me Back to Old Virginny" and "In the Evening By the Moonlight" are melodically superior and, at least lyrically equal to any song written by Stephen Collins Foster. The composer of these two songs was James A. Bland, the first Negro composer of note. It is evident that James Bland was influenced by the works of Foster, since the Foster style is apparent throughout.

In addition to Bland the famous minstrels, Bob Cole and Billy Johnson, authored "The Wedding of the Chinee and the Coon" in 1897. Later the songwriting team of Cole and J. Rosimond Johnson produced many hits. There was also a James Waldon Johnson who worked with this team. "Under the Bamboo Tree" was their greatest hit.

Gussie L. Davis was a kindred spirit of Paul Dresser in that he specialized in tear-jerkers. His work is a fine example of the capability of the Black man to equal song for song his white brother, be it ballad, spiritual or comic in character.

The songwriting teams of Bert Williams–George Walker, Alex Rogers–Will Marion Cooke, Henry Creamer–Turner Layton, and Charles Warfield–Clarence Williams, plus Ernest Hogan equal nine more Black composers of note. In addition

The Composers   are the many *rag* writers. (See Chapter 4, Hits Without Words and the Blues.)

William C. Handy, Duke Ellington, and Scott Joplin need little introduction here. Unlike James Bland, their reputations as composers are familiar to most. William C. Handy is the Father of the Blues; Duke Ellington's recent death saddened the world; and Scott Joplin's rags are being rediscovered and revived.

For William C. Handy and Scott Joplin songs, see Chapter 4.

Negro Composers and their song successes

James Bland

Carry Me Back to Ol' Virginny   1878
Close Dem Windows
De Golden Wedding   1880
Gabriel's Band
Hand Me Down My Walking Cane   1880
In the Evening By the Moonlight   1879
In the Morning By the Bright Light   1870
Listen to the Silver Trumpets
Oh, Dem Golden Slippers   1870
Pretty Little Carolina Rose
Tapioca
Travelin' Back to Alabam'
Way Up Yonder
You Could Have Been True

*Bob Cole and
the Johnsons*

Chicken (Billy Johnson and Accooe)   1899
Congo Love Song   1903
La Boola Boola (Billy Johnson)   1907
Lazy Moon   1903
Maiden with the Dreamy Eyes (J. Rosimond Johnson)   1901
My Castle on the Nile (J. Rosimond Johnson)   1901
Nobody's Lookin' but the Owl and the Moon (J. Rosimond Johnson)   1901
Oh! Didn't He Ramble   1902
Under the Bamboo Tree (J. Rosimond Johnson)   1902
The Wedding of the Chinee and de Coon (Billy Johnson)   1897

*Henry Creamer and
Turner Layton*

After You've Gone   1918
The Bombo Shay (With Henry Lewis)   1915
Dear Old Southland   1921
Down in the Borneo Isle

Henry Creamer and *Turner Layton (cont'd)*	Everybody's Crazy 'Bout the Doggone Blues, But I'm Happy 1917 Sweet Emalina, By Gal 1917 Way Down Yonder in New Orleans 1922
Gussie L. Davis	Beyond Pardon, Beyond Recall 1896 Down in Poverty Row (Music by Arthur Trevelyan) 1895 The Fatal Wedding (Words by Windom) 1893 Get on Your Sneak Shoes Children 1898 If I Could Blot Out the Past 1896 In the Baggage Coach, Ahead 1896 Light House by the Sea 1886 My Creole Sue 1898 Parted at the Altar 1895 Picture 84 (Words by Charles B. Ward) 1894 Wait till the Tide Comes in (Words by Joe Prophetes) 1887 When I Do the Hootchy Kootchy in the Sky 1896
Edward Kennedy *(Duke) Ellington*	Black and Tan Fantasy 1927 Blue Harlem 1935 Creole Rhapsody 1932 Don't Get Around Much Anymore (Words by Bob Russell) 1942 I Got It Bad and That Ain't Good 1941 I Let a Song Go out of My Heart 1943 In a Sentimental Mood 1935 It Don't Mean a Thing, If It Ain't Got That Swing 1932 Mood Indigo (Words by Irving Mills and Albany Bogard) 1931 Solitude (Words by Eddie De Lange and Irving Mills) 1934 Sophisticated Lady 1933
Bert Williams and *George Walker*	De Darkies Jubilee 1897 The Ghost of a Coon 1900 Nobody (Alex Rogers) 1905 She's Gettin More Like the White Folks Everyday The Voodoo Man

WOMEN COMPOSERS

Hattie Starr (the first successful woman composer), Charlotte Blake, Beth Slater Whitson, and Carrie Jacobs-Bond—a mere foursome represent the distaff side of Tin Pan Alley composers prior to 1920. Of these four, only Carrie Jacobs-Bond strikes a note of familiarity to the average individual.

Carrie Jacobs-Bond was an island unto herself as far as the music publishing business was concerned. Upon the death of her husband, Dr. Frank L. Bond, she supported herself and family by composing, printing, publishing, and as a vocalist, plugging her own songs. She has also been given credit for painting and designing her own song sheet covers.* This may very well be true on the unsigned covers, but her covers are also signed by the artists F. Hyer, George Hauman, and Marie Johnson. The Bond songs are recognizable on sight since they were printed on what is referred to as "linens"—an expensive and enduring paper with a minutely pebbled texture. (See Chapter 8, Special Covers.) The sole decoration normally consisted of a floral bouquet or garland of flowers.

The twenties saw Dorothy Fields and Mabel Wayne attain important stature as composers. Mabel Wayne composed the music for "Ramona" and "In a Little Spanish Town" plus many others. Dorothy Fields' superiority as a lyricist is a great testimonial to the ability of the female of the species. She displays none of the saccharine sentimentality evident in the works of her predecessors such as Carrie Jacobs-Bond or any of the moon-June platitudes that were a carryover into the twenties. Highly original and spirited, always tasteful, over the years the caliber of her lyrics has left little to be improved upon. The recent death of Dorothy Fields was mentioned during the 1974 Tony Awards presentation. She had contributed lyrics for a Tony nomination after fifty years as a successful songwriter!

There were dozens of women who participated occasionally as songwriters. To mention a few are Nora Bayes, May Irwin, Anita Owen, Clare Kummer, and Minnie Iris, but primarily it has been a field dominated by the male gender.

Song Samples

Charlotte Blake

The Harbor of Love (Words by Earl C. Jones)   1911
Land of Beautiful Dreams (Words by Maurice E. Marks)   1913
Love Ain't Likin', Likin' Ain't Love (Words by Earl C. Jones)   1910
Miss Coquette Waltzes   1910
A Night, a Girl, a Moon (Words by Davis and Gillespie)   1908

---

* Just prior to publication, a Carrie Jacobs-Bond song was discovered with Carrie Jacobs-Bond's initials in the floral bouquet of the cover. This proves without any doubt that she did decorate her own song sheet covers.

*Carrie Jacobs-Bond**	A Cottage in God's Garden 1917
	I Love You Truly 1906
	Just a Wearyin' for You 1901
	A Perfect Day 1910
Dorothy Fields†	Cuban Love Song (Music by Herbert Stolhart) 1931
	Exactly Like You (With Jimmy McHugh) 1930
	I'm in the Mood for Love (With Jimmy McHugh) 1935
	Lost in a Fog (Music by Jimmy McHugh) 1934
	On the Sunny Side of the Street (With Jimmy McHugh) 1930
Hattie Starr	Little Alabamy Coon 1893
	Ole Bossy Cow
	Somebody Loves Me (Not to be confused with George Gershwin's) 1894
Mabel Wayne	Chiquita (Words by L. Wolfe Gilbert) 1928
	Don't Wake Me Up (Words by L. Wolfe Gilbert) 1925
	In a Little Spanish Town (Words by Sam Lewis and Joe Young) 1926
	It Happened in Monterey (Words by Billy Rose) 1930
	Little Man You've Had a Busy Day (Words by Maurice Sigler and Al Hoffman) 1934
	Ramona (Words by L. Wolfe Gilbert) 1927
Beth Slater Whitson	Let Me Call You Sweetheart (Music by Leo Friedman) 1910
	Meet Me Tonight in Dreamland (Music by Leo Friedman) 1909
	One Sweetheart Is Enough For Me
	Tell Me That You Love Me (Music by Leo Friedman) 1912
	Yours Is Not the Only Aching Heart 1907

*Her songs number in the eighties.

†See also major composers with Jimmy McHugh.

CHAPTER 4

Hits
Without Words
and the Blues

Falling into the category of Hits without Words and the Blues are rags, cakewalks, marches, Indian intermezzos, hesitations, and all the subsequent dance styles from the foxtrot to the tango. Cake walks should be included even though lyrics accompanied the music on occasion.

Hits without words, as the term implies, encompass a broad variety of rhythms published mainly to perpetuate an unprecedented dance fever that began with ragtime. They were occasionally written with words, but more often than not, devoid of lyrics. The demand was overwhelming, and one wonders if this same demand for the dance superseded the ability of the lyric writers to keep pace.

They are divided into the following subcategories and consecutively enlarged upon: Cake walks, Rags, Foxtrots, Hesitation waltz (Boston), Indian intermezzos or ballads, Marches, and Blues.

CAKE WALKS

The period—the 1880s and 1890s. The dance—the cake walk. The association of the cake walk with a new rhythm called ragtime caused it to be an important milestone in the history of the dance. The cake walk was an exaggerated strut in which originally only Blacks participated. (The covers verify this since only Blacks seem to be represented thereon.) Later of course, "Everybody's Doin' It." The prize for the best performing couple was a cake—thus the title. The supply of cake walks is small, and the demand is large.

I may be criticized for including cake walks in a chapter about hits without words, because they were also sometimes written with lyrics. Here is a typical example of the difficulty encountered in categorizing.

Cake Walks

After the Cake Walk	Nathaniel Dett	1900
Alabama Cake Walk	George D. Barnard	1899
At a Darktown Cake Walk	Charles Hale	1897
At a Georgia Camp Meeting	Kerry Mills	1897
Aunt Dinah's Cake Walk	William Neidenhammer	1897
Bridal Cake Walk	Anthony L. Marish	1897

Bunch of Blackberries	Abe Holtzman	1899
The Cake Walk in the Sky	Ben Harney	1899
Cake Walk of the Day	Tony Stanford	1899
A Carolina Cake Walk	Max Dreyfus	1898
Carolina Cake Walk	George D. Mears	1899
Dusky Dudes Cake Walk	Jean Schwartz	1899
Eli Green's Cake Walk	Sadie Kominsky	1899
Golliwog's Cake Walk	Claude Debussey	1908
High Yellow Cake Walk	F. Henry Klickmann	1915
The Hottest Ever Cake Walk	Charles Brown and Joe O'Dea	1898
Jasper Jenkins, de Cake-Walking Coon	Henry P. Vogel	1898
Miss Brown's Cake Walk	Bert Williams	1896
Mississippi Side Step	Leo E. Berliner	1899
De Ole Time Cake Walk	W. Moody and Lee B. Grabbe	1898
Pious Peter Cakewalk	Egbert Van Alstyne	1898
Prancing Pickaninnies	Andrew Sterling and Max Dreyfus	1899
Prize Cake Walk of the Blackville Swells	Walter V. Uliner	1898
Salute to Sam Johnson (Cake Walk)	O. E. Sutton	1899
Sambo Outa Work Cake Walk	J. A. Silberberg	1899
Sister Kate Cake Walk	A. J. Piron	1919
Smokey Mokes	Abe Holzman	1899
Walkin' fo' dat Cake	Ed Harrigan and David Braham	1877
Walkin' fo' de Great White Cake	M. Petrousky	1898
Warm Proposition	Monroe Rosenfeld	1899

THOSE HEAVENLY RAGS!

In the cake walks was the embryo of a new rhythm called ragtime, which literally catapulted the nation into a dance craze that has never been equalled. By 1913 it was a full fledged mania, and the idols of the ballroom were the Irene and Vernon Castle and Maurice Mouret–Florence Walton dance teams. Although ragtime was an established rhythm many years prior to 1896, reputedly, the cake walks were the first published music in this rhythm. In ragtime the natural rhythm is distorted; the emphasis is on an unexpected beat. Said to have been spawned in brothels and honky tonks, it was not accepted by the class-conscious, but ragtime grew in spite of this. The people loved these lilting melodies with the crazy compelling beat.

Recognized as the foremost exponent of rags is Scot Joplin, a Black entertainer who wrote ragtime piano tunes. There were many others, such as James Scott, Joseph Lamb, Tom Turpin, Ben Harney, and Eubie Blake (who at 92, unbelievably, is still making personal appearances). The rags were written mainly *sans* lyrics, but who needed lyrics? The rags spoke a beautiful new language!

Credit for having written the first published, designated rag has been given to William Krell. His "Mississippi River" was published in 1897.

Hundreds and hundreds of rags were written by scores of writers. The now legendary Scott Joplin was a master of this musical cataclysm. He has been referred to as the Chopin of America, a fitting tribute to a highly talented Black man.

Leading all other categories in this area of song sheet collecting are rags. To own one rag is desirable; to own a collection is pure unsurpassed pleasure. Every title possible was used to name a rag. "Fuss and Feathers," "Chills and Fever," "Barbed Wire," "Holy Moses," and "Coal Smoke" are a few typical examples.

By the way, to you would-be rag collectors, "Alexander's Ragtime Band" by Irving Berlin is not a rag. Berlin contributed greatly to ragtime music with scores of rags, but this particular piece does not belong in a collection of rags.

The following song best expresses how completely ragtime captivated the public fancy.

I'm Certainly Living a Ragtime Life

WORDS BY Gene Jefferson   MUSIC BY Robert S. Robert

CHORUS

> I got a Ragtime dog and a Ragtime cat
> A Ragtime piano in my Ragtime flat
> Wear Ragtime clothes from hat to shoes
> I read a paper called the "Ragtime News"
> Got Ragtime habits and I talk that way,
> I sleep in Ragtime and I Rag all day
> Got Ragtime troubles with my Ragtime wife
> I'm certainly living a Ragtime life.

Copyright 1900 by Sol Bloom, New York, N. Y.

Introducing the Song Sheet

A warning: Unless you are prepared to spend more than a little time searching for rags, I would not advise anyone to buy Max Morath's superb rendition of Scott Joplin's and other rags, as featured on his Vanguard recording entitled "The Best of Scott Joplin." You just might end up catching a bad case of ragtime collector's fever. And there's no known cure!

Rags

Important rag writers are listed separately. Dates in all instances were not available.

Eubie Blake

Bugle Call Rag   1926
The Charleston Rag   1899
Chevy Chase   1914
Fizz Water   1914

George Botsford

Black and White Rag   1908
Chatterbox Rag   1910
The Grizzly Bear   1910
Hyacinth   1911

Charles L. Johnson

Apple Jack   1909
Crazy Bone Rag   1908
Dill Pickles   1906
Swanee Rag   1912

Scott Joplin

A Breeze From Alabama   1902
The Cascades (St. Louis World's Fair)   1904
The Chrysanthemum Rag   1904
Country Club   1909
Easy Winners   1901
Elite Syncopations   1902
The Entertainer   1903
Euphonic Sounds   1909
Felicity   1911 (Scott Hayden)
Fig Leaf   1908
Gladiolus Rag   1907
Heliotrope Bouquet (With Louis Chauvin)   1907
Kismet Rag (Scott Hayden)   1913
Maple Leaf Rag   1899
Original Rags   1899
Peacherine   1901
Pineapple Rag   1908

Scott Joplin (cont'd)	The Ragtime Dance	1906		
	A Real Slow Drag (Palm Leaf Rag)	1903		
	School of Ragtime	1908		
	Scott Joplin's New Rag	1912		
	Silver Swan (Attributed to Joplin)	1971		
	Solace	1909		
	Strenuous Life	1902		
	Sugar Cane	1908		
	Sunflower Slow Drag	1901 (Scott Hayden)		
	Swipsey Cake Walk	1900 (Arthur Marshal)		
	Wallstreet Rag	1909		

Joseph F. Lamb

American Beauty 1913
Champagne 1910
Ethiopa 1909
Excelsior Rag 1909
Sensation Rag 1908

James Scott

Climax Rag 1914
Dixie Dimples 1918
Frog Legs 1906
Grace and Beauty 1909
Hilarity 1910
Kansas City Rag 1907
Ophelia Rag
Princess Rag 1913
Quality Rag 1911
Ragtime Betty 1909
Sunburst Rag 1909

Tom Turpin

Bowery Buck 1899
Buffalo Rag 1904
Harlem Rag 1897
A Ragtime Nightmare 1900
St. Louis Rag (Fair) 1903

Others

African Pas'	Maurice Kerwin	1902
Alamo Rag	Wenrich and Deely	1910
All-of-a-Twist	Frank E. Hersom	1920
Angel Food Rag	Al Marzian	1911
Apple Sass	Harold Belding	1914
April Fool Rag	Jean Schwartz	1911
A Bag of Rags	W. R. Mackanlass	1912
Bell Hop Rag	Vera Maxwell and A. Braney	1914
Black and Blue Rag	Hal G. Nichols	1914

A Black Bawl	Harry C. Thompson	1905
Blue Goose Rag	Raymond Birch	1916
The Brownie Rag	Worster	1907
The Cabaret Rag	Joseph M. Daly	1913
Caberavings	Richard Whiting	1914
Calico Rag	Nat Johnson	1914
California Sunshine	Harry Jentis	1913
Calla Lily Rag	Logan Thane	1907
Candied Cherries	Lucien Denni	1911
Carbarlick Acid Rag	Clarence C. Wiley	1904
Castle House Rag	James Reese Europe	1914
Cataract Rag	Robert Hampton	1914
The Cauldron Rag	Wenrich and Christensen	1911
Chewin' the Rag	Fred Heltman	1912
Chills and Fever	Theron C. Bennett	1912
Coal Smoke	Clarence H. St. Johns	1904
Corrugated Rag	E. J. Mellinger	1911
Crabapples	Percy Wenrich	1918
Cracked Ice Rag	George L. Cobb	1918
Dakota Rag	O. H. Andersen	1899
Darktown Capers	Starck	
Dat Lovin' Rag	Smally and Odar	1908
Delightful Rag	Lester Sell	1914
The Dockstader Rag	Les Copeland	1912
Dope	W. C. Powell	1906
The Entertainers Rag	Jay Roberts	1912
Everybody Loves Rag	Dick Howard and A. Harriman	1914
Everybody's Rag	Dan Goldsmith and R. Sharp	1909
Freckles Rag	Larry Buck	1905
French Pastry Rag	Les Copeland	1914
Frozen Bill Rag	Arthur Pryor	
Fuss and Feathers	Morehead	
Glad Rags	Gould and Williams	1914
Gold Dust Twins Rag	Nat Johnson	1913
Good Gravy Rag	Harry Belding	1913
The Gravel Rag	Charlotte Blake	1908
Harmony Rag	Hal G. Nichols	1911
Holy Moses	C. Seymour	1906
Hot-House-Rag	Paul Pratt	1914
Humpty Dumpty	Charles Straight	1914
Hysterics Rag	Beise and Klickman	1914
Imperial Rag	Billie Talbot	1914
Intermission Rag	Charles Wellinger	1906
Jungle Jamboree Rag	Chris Smith	1913

The Junkman's Rag	C. Luckyth Roberts	1918
Lazy Luke	George L. Philpot	1905
Majestic Rag	Ben Rawls and Royal Neel	1914
Melody Rag	Raymond Birch	1911
Meteor Rag	Authur C. Morse	1920
The Midnight Whirl	Sylvio Hein	1914
Moose Rag	Ted Johnson	1910
Movie Rag	J. S. Zamecnik	1913
Music-Box-Rag	C. Luckyth Roberts	1914
Oceana Roll	Lucien Denni	1911
Oh That Navajo Rag	William and Van Alstyne	1911
Old Folks Rag	McCarthy and Goodwin	1913
Peaceful Henry	Harry Kelly	1901
Persian Lamb Rag	Percy Wenrich	1913
The Pipe Organ Rag	S. G. Rhodes	1912
Poverty Rag	Harry J. Lincoln	1909
The Rag of Rags Syncoper	William E. Macquinn	1915
Rag-Bag	Harry J. Lincoln	1909
Ragged Edges Rag	Otto Frey	1910
The Ragtime Violin	Irving Berlin	1911
Red Pepper	Henry Lodge	1910
The Red Rose Rag	Madden and Wenrich	1911
Saskatoon Rag	Phil Goldberg	1915
Seben Come Eleben	W. J. Bay	1899
Silver Fox	Henry Lodge	1915
Son of the Rag Time Boy	Sterling and Von Tilzer	1916
The Squirrel Rag	Paul Biese and Henri Klickman	1913
Steamboat Rag	Ernie Burnett	1914
Sympathetic Jasper	E. L. Catlin	1905
That Brass Band Rag	R. G. Grady	1912
That Fussy Rag	Victor H. Smalley	1910
That Gosh Darned Two-Step Rag	Kendrie and Miller	1913
That International Rag	Irving Berlin	1913
That Italian Rag	E. Leslie and A. Piantadosi	1910
That's-a-Plenty	Lew Pollack	1914
Tickle the Ivories	Wallie Herzer	1913
Tom Boy	W. F. Bradford	1901
Trilby Rag	Carey Morgan	1915
Turkish Towel Rag	Thomas S. Allen	1912
Wedding Bells Rag	A. B. Coney	1910

FOXTROTS

Ragtime had been a going concern since just before the turn of the century. Tin Pan Alley was now a full-fledged and thriving industry. As previously, it traversed the waves of all fads. The nation was obsessed with the dance; new dance creations were overnight sensations. Tin Pan Alley humbly and obediently complied to the demand, thereby enriching its coffers and assuring the perpetuation of the Alley.

As the supply of rags rapidly diminishes, a new source must tapped to satisfy the collectors under the Hits without words category. The foxtrot, lone survivor of the many dances named after the animal kingdom, is the logical successor to the rags. Like the rags, the foxtrots were titled with every name imaginable—"Frisky," "Dr. Brown," "Tiddledy Winks," "Reuben," "Cruel Papa," "Tickle Toes." The list is endless.

Thumbing through the foxtrots, one finds many ragtime luminaries—Lucky Roberts, Chris Smith, Charles L. Johnson, and Joe Jordon.

The artistry on the covers is outstanding. My advice is to collect while the foxtrots are still available.

Foxtrots

All Fussed Up	Richards and Pollack	1915
Ballin' the Jack	Chris Smith	1914
Beets and Turnips	Hess and Alhert	1915
By Heck	S. R. Henry	1914
Carolina Fox Trot	Will Vodery	1914
Cruel Papa	Will Marion Cooke	1914
Dicty-Doo	Carey Morgan	1914
Doctor Brown	Fred Irwin	1914
Frisky	Mel B. Kaufman	1919
Frou-Frou	Edward José	1915
Gee Whiz	Abe Losch	1919
The Hunt Club	Theo O. Taubert	1915
Meadowbrook Fox Trot	Arthur Kraus	1914
The Irish Fox Trot	Paul Biese	1915
The Kangaroo Hop	Kahn and Morris	1914
Let's Go	Charley Straight	1915
Marine Fox-Trot	Robert Marine	1915
Palm Beach	C. Luckyth Roberts	1914
Reuben Fox-Trot	Ed Claypoole	1914
Saddle-de-Mooch	Chris Smith	1915

Sam Fox Trot	George P. Howard	1915
Shakesperian Love	Hugo Frey	1914
The Sparkling Trot	L. L. Lynde	1914
Sugar Lump	Frederick Bryan	1914
Sweetie Dear	Joe Jordon	1914
Tambourine and Oranges	F. Henry Klickman	1915
That Raggy Foxtrot	Laurence E. Goffen	1915
Tickle Toes	William H. Penn	1914
Tiddle-de-Winks	Melville Morris	1916
The Tremolo Trot	C. Luckyth Roberts	1914

HESTITATIONS (BOSTON)

The waltz, once considered suggestive and indecent, had for decades past settled down to a position of respectability—a paragon of propriety. By the late 1900s, the boredom of the incessant 1—2—3—rhythm was more than a lively, impatient nation would condone. The tempo of the country had quickened; by now the automobile, telephone, and telegraph were an established way of life. An impetuous and proud U. S. A. in a new century had little, if anything, in common with the staid old country–originated waltz. It finally gave way to the foxtrots, the one-steps, and the two-steps, that is, up to a point. At this point some enterprising individual, perhaps reluctant to see the waltz fade into obscurity, modified the step and dubbed it the "hesitation" or "Boston." Revitalized, it was again a contending dance rhythm. Hesitations were written expressly for the dance idols of the day, such as the "Lame Duck" hesitation for Irene and Vernon Castle and "The Maurice" hesitation for Maurice Mouret of the Mouret and Florence Walton team. There were others too.

Unlike the rags and trots, the waltz never fell prey to humorous and occasionally ludicrous titles. She was a lady, and hesitated, syncopated, or whatever, she would remain so. "Waltz Elaine," "Waltz Brune," "Old Fashioned Roses," "Love Thoughts," "Yes and No Valse," and "Valse June"—all hesitations are typical. The covers, in keeping with the titles, were well within the borders of respectability. A touch of humor here and there, interesting, artistic but never (well, hardly ever) comical.

Hesitations **(Boston)**	Daddy Long Legs	Clarence M. Jones	1914
	Dreaming	Archibald Joyce	1911
	Geraldine	Henry Lodge	1915
	Half and Half	F. Henry Klickman	1914
	Illusion	L. Wolfe Gilbert and Carlo Neve	1914
	Just a Moment!	Egbert Van Alstyne	1914
	Le Poeme	Sigmund Romberg	1913
	One Wonderful Night	Clarence M. Jones	1914
	Pauline Waltz	Clarence M. Jones	1914
	Valse Brune	George Krier	1910
	Valse Elaine	Lionel Baxter	1915
	Valse June	Lionel Baxter	1914
	Valse Mauve	Will Wood (Arranger)	1914
	Waltz Irresistible	Anita Owen	1916
	Yes or No	Clarence M. Jones	1914

MISCELLANEOUS DANCES

In the collecting field, there is a certain amount of snob appeal attached to rarity or the unobtainables, which cannot be denied. The rags (categorically, the rag is not a dance) are rapidly approaching this status. Foxtrots and hesitations will more than likely follow suit in the not-too-distant future. The astute collector with an eye for investment will look to the still obtainable miscellaneous dances. The one-steps and two-steps are numerous.

This presents a problem of sorts because of the following: To take advantage of the public's varied taste in the dance, it was a common practice by the publishers to advertise a particular song as suitable for several different dances or rhythms. A typical example is "Tangomania," which could be a one- and two-step or tango. How does one determine which dance step takes precedence over another? The logical conclusion is that the dance step named in the title, regardless of what additional dances are mentioned, would be the correct classification. To add to this, the first mentioned dance would take priority. With this in mind, "You pays your money, you takes your choice."

For further diversification, a variety of dances could prove to be a most interesting collection. Under this category would fall the one-steps, two-steps, tangos, turkey trot, kangaroo dip, fish walk, Texas Tommy, the snake, crab step, grizzly bear, the airplane dip, and the waltzes—syncopated or hesitated. There are surely many others.

One- or Two-Steps	Cannon Ball	Joseph C. Northup	1905
	Captain Betty	Lionel Baxter	1914
	Cup Hunters	Julius Lenzberg	1915
	Fu	George P. Howard	1919
	Great Snakes!	Ernest Reeves	1911
	Melody Maids	W. Leon Ames	1914
	Ole Virginny	J. S. Zamecnik	1916
	Pepperpot	Harold Iver	1913
	Pink Poodle	Charles L. Johnson	1914
	Silhouette One Step	Harold Bien	1914
	Thanks for the Lobster	Clarence Jones	1914
	Tsin Tsin Ta Tao	D. Onivas	1914
	Yo San	Al W. Brown	1914
	Zum	Don Richardson	1915
Tangos	El Irrisistible	Egbert Van Alstyne	1914
	Everybody Tango	Paul Pratt	1914
	Pass the Pickles	Grace LeBoy	1913
	Tangomania	Egbert Van Alstyne	1914
	Tom Tom	Rosardios Furnari	1914

INDIAN INTERMEZZOS AND BALLADS

Because communication is the key to fad, Americans, who are superior to all others in this area, have the most fad-prone culture on earth. In 1903 "Navajo," by Williams and Van Alstyne, started just such another rage.

Baffling to me from the very beginning is the term "intermezzo." Webster's definition is, "a short, independent instrumental musical composition." But it seemed to be reserved almost solely for music pertaining to the American Indian. "Silver Heels," "Red Wing," "Fawneyes," "Morning Star," "Red Man," "Anona," "Golden Arrow," "Iola," "Moon Bird," and others were published as Indian intermezzos. If any degree of popularity was attained, lyrics were added and the songs became ballads. Why not more Italian, Hawaiian, or Irish intermezzos? My guess is this. Tin Pan Alley never rocked the boat of success. If a particular Indian song called an intermezzo became popular, the songwriters and publishers would produce as many Indian songs—calling them intermezzos—as the traffic would bear, or until the ear-weary public could tolerate no more of the same.

Whether it be basketry, rugs, or pottery, the Indian category is always a popular field of collecting. The Indian song sheet covers are extraordinarily attractive. The cover artists seemed to take special pains with the Indian maidens, who more often than not graced the covers.

The best loved Indian songs of all time is, I believe, "Red Wing." Its first publication date was 1907; the composers were Kerry Mills and Thurland Chattaway. A resurgence of popularity in 1932 was responsible for its reissue at that time. This could be one of the first examples of a Tin Pan Alley era song revival.

Indian intermezzos and ballads

Anona	Vivian Grey (Mabel McKinley)	1903
Fawneyes	Charles L. Johnson	1908
Hiawatha	Neil Moret	1902
Hiawatha's Melody of Love	Bryan, Mehlinger, and Meyer	1920
Hobomoko	Ernest Reeves	1907
Indian Love Call	Harbach, Oscar Hammerstein II, and Rudolph Friml	1924
Indian Lullaby	Glick and Wilson	1925
Indianola	S. R. Henry and Onivas	1918
Iola	James O'Dea	1906
Kachina-Hopi Girl's Dance	Albert Van Sand and Arthur Green	1914
Kissamee	J. S. Zamecnik	1914
Moon Dear	Egan, Whiting, and Moret	1905
Navajo	Williams and Van Alstyne	1903
Oh! That Navajo Rag	Williams and Van Alstyne	1911
Pretty Little Rainbow	Plunkett and Levenson	1919
Rainbow	Johnson and Wenrich	1908
Red Wing	Mills and Chattaway	1907
Seattle	Walter Augustyne	1909
Seminola	King and Warren	1925
Silver Bell	Madden and Wenrich	1910
Silver Heels	Neil Moret	1905

MARCHES

Marches were written for every conceivable event. Coming quickly to mind are inaugurals, expositions, political campaigns, and wars.

The name of John Philip Sousa is representative of the best in musical contributions to our American heritage. Appropriately dubbed the "March King," he is credited with over one hundred fifty marches. Probably never before or ever again will anyone equal the melodic and lilting swing of a "Sousa" march. They were *solid* hits. "Washington Post," "Stars and Stripes Forever," "Semper Fidelis," and "Liberty Bell" are known to nearly all.

Scores of march composers, including many stellar contributors, were part of the Tin Pan Alley scene. E. T. Paull marches, because of their spectacular lithographed covers, have been placed under Chapter 7, Special Covers. In addition, Harry J. Lincoln, J. S. Jamecnik, Paul Lincke, and George Rosey (G. M. Rosenberg) are representative of the better known march composers. Harry J. Lincoln was responsible for an endless list of marches. George Rosey's "Honeymoon" and "Anniversary" marches were hits of the day circa 1895.

After the turn of the century, the march music was published with colorful covers encompassing a variety of subjects. They are excellent sources for photographs of presidents, catastrophes, and news events.

Marches

J. S. Jamecnik

All America March   1916
Co-ed March   1914
College Yell March   1908
World Peace March   1914

Harry J. Lincoln

Baldwin Commandery   1906
A Jolly Sailor   1908
Midnight Fire Alarm   1900
Observatory
Old Hickory   1913
The Palm Limited   1905
Peace Conference   1915
The Rifle Range   1907
Sounds from the Orient   1906

Harry J. Lincoln (cont'd)	Steeple Chase 1914
	Susquehanna
	Tri-State 1906
	United Musicians 1915
	Vesuvius

George (G. M. Rosenberg) Rosey	The Anniversary 1895
	The Chinatown March
	The Handicap March
	The Honeymoon 1895
	King Carnival March
	Oriental Echoes March

John Philip Sousa	America First 1916
	The Atlantic City Pageant 1927
	Century of Progress (Chicago World's Fair) 1931
	Custer's Last Charge
	El Capitan 1895
	George Washington Bicentennial 1930
	The Honored Dead (U. S. Grant) 1896
	Imperial Edward Military March (Dedicated to Edward VII)
	King Cotton (Official march of Atlantic Exposition) 1904
	Liberty Bell 1895
	Liberty Loan 1917
	Magna Charta 1927
	The National Game (Dedicated to baseball's Landis)
	Semper Fidelis 1888
	Sesqui-Centennial Exposition of U. S. 1921
	Stars and Stripes Forever 1897
	The Thunderer 1889
	U. S. Field Artillery 1917
	Washington Post March 1889

Miscellaneous

American Patrol	F. W. Meacham	1895
Boots and Saddles	Glen W. Ashley	1910
Brown's Jubilee March	Samuel D. Brown	1881
Creole Belles	J. Bodewalt Lampe	1900
Cuban Independence	C. D. Henninger	1898
The Fireman's Dream	Percy Wenrich	1907
Flipity Flop	L. H. Dougherty	1901
The Fox Hunter's March	William H. Penn	1900
Imperial March and Two Step	Newton B. Heims	1915
Jasper's Triumphal March	C. M. Vandersloot	1914
Loyal Knights	F. H. Losey	1907

Salute to Williamsburg	C. E. Duble	1906
Soldiers of Fortune	L. O. Gustin	1901
Somethin' Doin'	F. H. Losey	1907
Triumphant America	F. H. Losey	1907
Wayside Willies March	Charles L. Johnson	1905
The Whip	Abe Holzman	1913
The Woodrow Wilson Inaugural	Jacques Hertz	1913
Yankiana	E. E. Loftis	1905

THE BLUES

W. C. Handy's 1911 publication of "The Memphis Blues" was a harbinger of things to come in the realm of music.

The expression of despair and discontent has a tendency to relieve these feelings, and so the downtrodden Negroes vented their sorrows by singing the blues (a twelve-bar refrain with flatted thirds and sevenths). They captivated the nation's fancy, and soon the entire populace sang along.

Mr. Handy, known as the "Father of the blues," Duke Ellington, Jelly Roll Morton, and Fats Waller were all stellar contributors to this musical medium. Of course all songwriters climbed aboard the "blues" wagon, and like the rags many non-blues masqueraded under the blues title. Nonetheless Tin Pan Alley thereby profited immensely. The blues retained their popularity well into the post–Tin Pan Alley era.

Blues singers Gertrude "Ma" Rainey and her understudy Bessie Smith, have gained permanent and esteemed places in the archives of Tin Pan Alley.

There were several blues styles evolving from primitive blues. For this reason I will not attempt to differentiate between genuine blues songs and songs with "blues" in the title. This I leave to the musicologists. Like the rags and trots, blues number in the hundreds.

Blues

W. C. Handy

Atlanta Blues   1924
Aunt Agar Blues   1920
The Basement Blues   1924
Beale St. Blues   1916
Blue Gummed Blues   1926
East of St. Louis Blues   1937

W. C. Handy (cont'd)	Friendless Blues	1926
	Golden Brown Blues	1927
	Hesitating Blues	1915
	Joe Turner Blues	1915
	Jogo Blues	1903
	John Henry Blues	1922
	Loveless Love Blues	1921
	Memphis Blues	1912
	St. Louis Blues	1914
	Sundown Blues	1923
	Wall St. Blues	1929
	Yellow Dog Blues	1914

Others

The Alcoholic Blues	Edward Laska and Albert Von Tilzer	1919
All Alone Again Blues	Jerome Kern	1920
Barnyard Blues		1918
Basin Street Blues	Spencer William	1933
Blame It on the Blues	Charles L. Cooke	1914
Bow Wow Blues	Friend and Osborne	1922
Bye Bye Blues	Fred Hamm, Dave Bennett, Bert Lown, and Chauncey Grey	1930
Don't Take Away Those Blues	Joe McKiernan and Norman Spencer	1920
Doo Dah Blues	Billy Rose and Ted Fiorito	1922
I've Got the Right to Sing the Blues	Hoagy Carmichael	1932
I've Got the Yes! We Have No Bananas Blues	Brown, Hanley, and King	1923
Jimmies Mean Mamma Blues	Jimmy Rodgers, Walter O'Neal, and Bob Sawyer	1931
Kentucky Blues	Clarence Gaskill	1921
Limehouse Blues	Furber and Brobom	1924
Lonesome Mama Blues	A. Brown, Nickel, and B. Brown	1922
Pickaninny Blues	McKiernan	1924
Pickaninny Waltz Lullaby Blues	Harold Frost and F. Henry Klickmann	1919
Promise Me Everything, Never Get Anything Blues	Pease and Nelson	1924
Rock-a-Bye My Baby Blues	Billy Hill and Larry Yoell	1921
Sugar Blues	Fletcher and Williams	1923
Take 'Em to the Door Blues	Billy Rose, Benny Davis, and Ray Henderson	1925
Travelling Blues	Russell and Bergman	1924
Wang Wang Blues	Mueller, Johnson, and Henry Busse	1921
Yankee Doodle Blues	George Gershwin	1923

CHAPTER 5

Miscellaneous Categories

TEAR-JERKERS

It is a paradox that during the so-called Gay Nineties—although factually beginning in the 1880s and lasting well into the 1900s—the song style that held the country completely in sway was what is now referred to as the tear-jerkers. It was the tragic opera of Tin Pan Alley. The very fact that the public associated itself so completely with the lachrymose ballads casts suspicion on the credibility of the term Gay Nineties (realistically there must have been some basis for this title). Perhaps a desire to emulate gaiety was a nation's attempt at playing the clown, of covering up the heartaches and injustices caused by the ineptitude of existing laws, the too rigid moral codes, and a high mortality rate. For whatever reasons, the people were obsessed with the sob songs, and songwriters and publishers obliged by pouring forth a constant stream of tragedies set to music.

The songwriter of "Banks of the Wabash" fame, whose own life paralleled the teary songs he composed in quantity, was the famous Paul Dresser, brother of the novelist Theodore Dreiser. The family name Dreiser was changed to Dresser by Paul. He literally died of a broken heart, forsaken by associates whom he befriended generously during his lucrative years as songwriter and publisher. Broke and unable to convince the doubting publishers that "My Gal, Sal" was a potential hit, he died prior to its publication. With the exception of "Banks of the Wabash," it was perhaps his greatest song. He considered it so.

Tear-Jerkers

Paul Dresser

The Convict and the Bird   1888
Don't Tell Her That You Saw Me   1896
I Wonder Where She Is Tonight   1899
Just Tell Them That You Saw Me   1895
The Letter That Never Came   1886
The Outcast Unknown   1887
The Pardon That Came Too Late   1891

Ed Marks and Joe Stern

Break The News to Mother Gently   1892
Don't Wear Your Heart on Your Sleeve   1901
His Last Thoughts Were of You   1894
The Little Lost Child   1894

| *Ed Marks and* | My Mother Was a Lady | 1896 | |
| *Joe Stern (cont'd)* | The Old Postmaster | 1900 | |

Others

After the Ball	Charles K. Harris	1892
At a Cost of a Woman's Heart	Carter and Braisted	1907
The Baggage Coach Ahead	Gussie L. Davis	1906
Break the News to Mother	Charles K. Harris	1897
Cradle's Empty—Baby's Gone	Harry Kennedy	1880
For Sale—a Baby	Charles K. Harris	1903
Hello Central Give Me Heaven	Charles K. Harris	1901
In the City Where Nobody Cares	Charles K. Harris	1910
In the Heart of the City That Has No Heart	Allen and Daly	1913
In the House of Too Much Trouble	Heelan and Helf	1900
The Letter Edged in Black	Hattie Nevada	1897
The Poor Little Rich Girl	Caddigan and Pressman	1914
She Is More to be Pitied Than Censored	W. B. Grey	1898
She's Only a Bird in a Gilded Cage	Lamb and Harry Von Tilzer	1900
Since Nellie Went Away	Joseph Skelley	1892
Stay in Your Own Back Yard	Kennet and Udall	1899
There's No More Buster Brown	Breen and Conlon	1908
Two Little Girls in Blue	Charles Graham	1893
When We Were Two Little Boys	Madden and Morse	1904
Why Did They Dig Ma's Grave So Deep?	Joseph Skelley	1880

ALCOHOL AND PROHIBITION

"Cradle's Empty—Baby's Gone," a popular tear-jerker, was too inviting to let slip by. "Bottle's Empty, Whiskey's Gone" was the followup. "You'll Never Miss the Water Till the Well Runs Dry" was countered with "You'll Never Miss the Lager Till the Keg Runs Dry." These irreverent parodies are indicative of the Victorian's humorous attitude toward Demon Rum.

The spectacle of an individual drinking himself into insensibility does not in this enlightened age evoke the guffaws of laughter so often depicted in the past in song and story. The subject of alcoholism was treated as unmitigated mirth or stark tragedy and in either case was a popular vehicle for songwriters.

The influence Tin Pan Alley had on the consumption of alcohol is incalculable, but judging by the number of songs associated with the bottle, it was most emphatically a highly esteemed commodity. Did Tin Pan Alley plant the seeds of

Prohibition? This is doubtful, but it certainly nurtured them, with the "Father, Dear Father, Come Home With Me Now" type of tear-jerker.

In any event, alcoholism and Prohibition are facets of life in these United States and another field for the collector.

Alcohol and Prohibition Songs

Bitter Beer		
Bottle's Empty, Whiskey's Gone		
Brown October's Ale	Smith and De Koven	1890
Budweiser's a Friend of Mine	Bryan and Furth	1907
Casey's Whiskey		1878
Champagne Charlie		
Champagne Song		
Connect Me With the Brewery		
Curious Cures	James Thornton	1897
Down Where the Wurzeburger Flows	Bryan; Harry Von Tilzer	1902
Drinking Song		
The Drunkard's Wife		
Empty Is the Bottle, Father's Tight	Walter Delaney	1878
Everybody Wants a Key to My Cellar	Rose, Backett, and Pollock	1919
Glorious Beer, Beer, Glorious Beer	Leggett and Goodwin	1895
Heidleberg Stein Song	Pixley and Luder	1902
I Never Drink Behind the Bar	Harrigan and Braham	1883
Ida, Sweet as Apple Cider	Eddie Leonard	1903
If I Meet the Guy Who Made This Country Dry		
I'm on the Water Wagon Now	West and Bratton	1903
It Will Never Be Dry Down in Havana		
I've Been Floating Down That Old Green River	Bert Kalmar and Joe Cooper	1915
King Highball		
Little Brown Jug	Eastburn	
Maine Stein Song		
Malone at the Back of the Bar	Harrigan and Braham	1875
Pitcher of Beer	Harrigan and Braham	1880
Prohibition Blues	Ring Lardner and Nora Bayes	1919
Sabel's Sparkling Champagne Song	Josie Sabel	1894
Show Me the Way to Go Home	Irving King	1925
What'll We Do on a Saturday Night When the Town Goes Dry	Bert Kalmar and Harry Ruby	1919
When I Took the Keeley Cure	James Thornton	
You Never Miss the Lager Till the Keg Runs Dry	Gus Williams	

FOOD AND NONALCOHOLIC BEVERAGES

There is not a thing in today's diet-prone culture to inspire the writing of a hit song. "A Diet Drink, a Frozen Dinner and You" ("A Cup of Coffee, a Sandwich and You") would hardly give rise to a feeling of exultation or stimulate one to create.

But oh! The good old days when, without feelings of recrimination, one could indulge in his favorite fare, be it "Hot Chocolate," "Plum Pudding," or "Citron Wedding Cake" (typical food-associated song titles). To partake of such a fattening diet now is unthinkable, much less setting it to music.

Today's permissive society, strangely enough, does not include food. Morality regarding its consumption never enjoyed such high standards. Promiscuous indulgence in food is absolutely condemned. Happily such gratification was immortalized in song years ago, and although we are forbidden to sate ourselves with these delicacies, we are still free to sing about them and to collect the song sheets.

Food and Nonalcoholic Beverage Songs

Ada, My Sweet Patata		
Bake Dat Chicken Pie	Frank Dumont	1906
Big Rock Candy Mountain		
Blueberry Hill	Stock, Lewis, and V. Rose	1940
Bunch of Berries		
Candy	Joan Whitney and Alex Kramer	1945
Cherry Ripe		
Chili Bean	Lew Brown and Albert Von Tilzer	1920
Chiquita Banana		
Cocoanuts		
A Cup of Coffee, a Sandwich and You	Billy Rose, Al Dubin, and Joe Meyer	1925
Cup of Tea		
Dat Citron Wedding Cake	Harrigan and Braham	1880
Down Among the Sugar Cane	McPherson and Smith	1908
Gee, But I Like Music With My Meals	Seymour Brown and Nat D. Ayer	1911
Ginger Blues	Harrigan and Braham	1876
He Knows His Groceries	Lou Breau	1926
Hot Chocolate		
Hot Tamale Alley	George M. Cohan	1896
Ida, Sweet as Apple Cider	Eddie Leonard	1903
I'm Putting All My Eggs in One Basket	Irving Berlin	1935
The Last Cake of Supper		

Lemon in the Garden of Love	Rourke and Carle	1906
Let's Have Another Cup of Coffee	Irving Berlin	1932
Life Is Just a Bowl of Cherries	Brown and Henderson	1931
Macaroni Joe	Stanley Murphy and Percy Wenrich	1910
Not for All the Rice in China		
On the Good Ship Lollipop	Sydney Clare and Richard Whiting	1934
Oyster, a Cloister and You	Richard Connels	1925
Peanut Vendor	El Manisero	
Real Nice Clambake		
Tea for Two	Harbach, Ceasar and Youmans	1925
Won't You Come to My Teaparty	Alb. H. Fitz	1896
Yes, We Have No Bananas	F. Silver and Irving Cohen	1923
You're the Cream in My Coffee	DeSylva, Brown, and Henderson	1928

Rags and Miscellaneous Dance Food Songs

Angel Food (Rag)
Apple Sass (Rag)
Beets and Turnips (Foxtrot)
Candied Cherries (Rag)
Crabapples (Rag)
Dill Pickles (Rag)
French Pastry (Rag)
Good Gravy (Rag)
Pass the Pickles (Tango)
Pepper Pot (One-step)
Red Pepper (Rag)
Sugar Lump (Foxtrot)
Tambourines and Oranges (Foxtrot)
Thanks for the Lobster (One-step)

WEARING APPAREL

The one outstanding article of clothing featured on song sheets is "The Big Beautiful Hat," which enjoyed popularity between 1890 and 1910. One can wax lyrical over these superb creations. They were thoughtfully fashioned to accommodate the up-sweep and Gibson girl hairdos of the day. "Bird on Nellie's Hat," "San Francisco, the Paris of the U. S. A.," "Oh You Beautiful Doll," and "Keep Your Foot on the Soft Pedal" are prized examples from my own collection.

In addition to the hats are bustles, bloomers, pinafores, sunbonnets, peg-bottom trousers, derbies, racoon coats, *ad infinitum*. "The Ra Ra Boy" boasts pegged trousers reminiscent of Zoot Suiters of the 1940s—this back in 1914!

Predating Tin Pan Alley is "Dressed in a Dolly Varden."

Introducing the
Song Sheet

Postdating it is "My Little Yellow Polka-dot Bikini." The old saw that clothes make the man might be rephrased to read: What becomes a part of him, man forms an attraction for. Wearing apparel, a necessary commodity, is always subject to periodic changes at the command of the style setters. These passing fancies of fashion provided fuel for Tin Pan Alley's eternal fires, so if Paris dictated, the Alley perpetuated.

A framed collection of song sheets depicting fashion or about fashion would result in a style show that would be the envy of all who would view.

Wearing Apparel Songs

Alice Blue Gown	McCarthy and Tierny	1919
All Around My Hat		
Baby Shoes		
Bandana Days	Noble Sissler and Eubie Blake	1921
Bandana Land	Victor Herbert	1906
The Beautiful Lady in Blue	Lewis and Coots	1935
Bell Bottom Trousers	Moe Joffe	1943
Big Red Shawl	Cole and Johnson	1908
Bloomer Girl	Arlen and Harburg	1944
Button up Your Overcoat	DeSylva, Brown, and Henderson	1928
The Faded Coat of Blue	J. H. McNaughton	1865
Fella With an Umbrella	Irving Berlin	1948
Gal in Calico	Leo Robbins and Arthur Schwartz	1946
Get on Your Sneak Shoes Children	Gussie L. Davis	1898
The Gingham Girl	Fleeson; Albert Von Tilzer	
Green Hat	Scholl, Browne, and Rich	1933
Hat Me Father Wore	Ferguson and McCarthy	1878
The Hat Me Father Wore on St. Patrick's Day	William Jerome and Arthur Schwartz	1909
Hats Make the Woman	Victor Herbert	1905
Hats Off to Me	Harrigan and Braham	1890
Keep Your Skirts Down, Maryanne	King, Sterling, and Henderson	1925
The Lady in Red	Dixon and Wrubel	1935
Let a Smile Be Your Umbrella	Irving Kahal and Francis Wheeler	1927
Let Me Bring My Clothes Back Home	Irving Jones	1898
Little Empty Stockings	Harry Kennedy	1883
Little Shawl of Blue	Hewitt and Teschmacher	1913
My Gal in the Guinea Blue Gown	R. Emmet Kennedy	
My Old Scarlet Coat		
One, Two, Button Your Shoe	John Burke and Arthur Johnson	1936

Put My Little Shoes Away	Mitchell and Pratt	1873
Put on Your Old Grey Bonnet	Stanley Murphy and Percy Wenrich	
The Silver Slipper		
Sunbonnet Sue	Will D. Cobb and Gus Edwards	1908
Top Hat, White Tie and Tails	Irving Berlin	1935
Where Did You Get That Hat?	Joseph J. Sullivan	1886
Who Threw the Overalls in Mrs. Murphy's Chowder?	George L. Geifer	1899

LOCATIONS

Judging by a colossal number of songs, Heaven is right here on earth with two geographical locations. One is lovingly referred to as Dixie. The other is that super-green isle of Erin. These sections of real estate have been romanticized, eulogized, memorialized, and set to music more than all other places combined, with the exception of Hawaii. Our island state falls not *too* far behind.

One could speculate forever on why the South has been treated with such tuneful reverence. Whatever the reason, it was the public's wish and Tin Pan Alley's command. There is a natural interrelationship between Dixie and coon songs, each category often encompassing the other. If the song is about Dixie as a location, it should probably be classified as such. Again, if the subject of the song is "coon," even though the location is Dixie, it would fall into the "coon" category.

The influx of Irish immigrants during the latter half of the nineteenth century had a profound effect on the citizenry, capturing hearts with ever-present broguish wit, sentimentality, and Irish shenanigans. People sing about what moves them deeply. The Harrigan-Hart team and their variety shows of the 1880s are testimony to the feelings Americans had toward the Irish. Irish in substance and song, these plays were tremendously successful. From that time forward, as with Dixie, the Emerald Isle and its inhabitants kept the songwriters busy. A lot of that green rubbed right off on the Tin Pan Alley publishers in the form of dollar bills!

Nearly every state and major city can boast at least one song title containing its name. Rivers, mountains, and streets were also grist for the mill of sentimentality. Broadway was a favorite, as was the Mississippi River. Paul Dresser's "Banks of the Wabash" is highly esteemed, and James Bland's "Carry Me

Back to Old Virginny" became Virginia's official state song in 1956.

If you are a globe trotter at heart, the location category would most certainly suit your personality.

Dixie

Should you have *purist* inclinations, only songs with *Dixie* in the title would be of interest to you, but of course Dixie encompassed the entire area south of the Mason-Dixon line. Whether one choses to exclude the hundreds of songs of the Southland devoid of Dixie in the title is a personal matter. I am not listing them here, since so many were about the individual states and have been dealt with elsewhere. Many also were about rivers like the Swanee and Wabash.

Dixie Songs

Ain't You Coming Back to Dixieland?		
Alexander's Band Is Back in Dixieland	Yellen; Gumble	1919
All Aboard for Dixie	Jack Yellen; George L. Cobb	1913
Are You From Dixie	Jack Yellen; George L. Cobb	1915
Back to Dixieland	Jack Yellen	1914
Dancing Down in Dixieland		
Dixie Land, I Love You	A. S. Hayer; Nat Brown	1909
Anything Is Nice If It Comes from Dixieland	Clarke; Meyer; Ager	1919
Goodbye Dixie Goodbye	Trace; Mohr	1920
Happy Days in Dixie	Kerry Mills	1896
How's Every Little Thing in Dixie	Jack Yellen; Albert Gumble	1916
I Want to Be in Dixie	Berlin; Snyder	1912
I'm All Bound 'Round With the Mason-Dixon Line	Lewis; Young; Schwartz	1917
In Dixie Land with Dixie Lou	Drislane; Meyer	1912
Is It True What They Say About Dixie?	Irving Ceaser; Sam Lerner; Gerry Marks	1936
It's a Hundred to One You're from Dixie	L. Wolfe Gilbert; Harry Morgan	1917
Listen to That Dixie Band	Jack Yellen; George L. Cobb	1914
Moonlight Down in Dixie	Sym. Winkle; Jack Kalin	1919
Rockabye Your Baby With a Dixie Melody	Jerome; Schwartz	1918
She's Dixie All the Time	A. Bryan; Tierney	1916
She's the Fairest Little Flower Dear Old Dixie Ever Knew		
There's a Lump of Sugar Down in Dixieland	Bryan; Yellen; Gumble	1918
They Made It Twice as Nice as Paradise and They Called It Dixieland	Ramond Egan; Richard Whiting	1916
When It's Nighttime Down in Dixieland	Irving Berlin	1914

When the Sun Goes Down in Dixie	Charles McCarron; Albert Von Tilzer	1917
The Whole World Comes From Dixie		

Songs about Ireland

Along the Rocky Road to Dublin	Young; Grant	1915
Erin's Isle and You	J. R. Shannon; J. S. Zamecnik	1914
Farewell Killarney		
For Freedom and Ireland	Woodward; Mack	1900
I Dreamed That Old Ireland Was Free		
I Love You Kate in Ireland	Edwin French	1890
I'm on My Way to Dublin Bay	Stanley Murphey	1915
Ireland Is Ireland to Me	Fiske O'hara; J. K. Brennan; E. Ball	1915
Ireland Must Be Heaven for My Mother Came from There	McCarthy; H. Johnson; Fisher	1916
Ireland Never Seemed So Far Away		
Irishman's Home Sweet Home	Felix McGlennon	1880's
Just Sing a Song for Ireland	A. Sterling; H. Von Tilzer	1898
Killarney My Home o'er the Sea	Frederick Knight Logan	1911
Lass From County Mayo	Raymond A. Browne	1897
Letter From Ireland	J. F. Mitchell	1886
A Little Bit of Heaven and They Called It Ireland	J. Keirn Brennan; Ernest Ball	1914
Little Town in the Old County Down	Pasco; Carlo; Sanders	1920
My Own Home Town in Ireland	Bartly Costello; Alfred Solman	1915
Roses of Picardy	Weatherly; Wood	1916
She's Never Been in Ireland But She's Irish Just the Same	Shields; Mack	1911
Sweet Iniscarra	Chauncey Olcott	1897
Sweet Rose of Athlone		
That Tumble Down Shack in Athlone	R. W. Pascoe; Monte Carlo; Alma M. Sanders	1918
When It's Moonlight in Mayo		
When Shall I Again See Ireland	Blossom; Herbert	1917
Where the River Shannon Flows	James I. Russell	1906
You'll Find a Little Bit of Ireland Everywhere		

Songs about Hawaii

Blue Hawaii	Leo Robins; Ralph Rainger	1937
Hawaiian Bluebird	Morgan	1919
Hawaiian Butterfly	George A. Little; Billy Baskette; Joe Santly	1907
Hawaiian Moonlight	Harold G. Frost; F. Henri Klickman	1908
Hawaiian Nights		
Hawaiian Sunshine	L. Wolfe Gilbert; Carey Morgan	1917

Hawaiian Twilight	Herbert B. Marple	1918
Hello, Hawaii, How Are You?	Bert Kalmar; Edgar Leslie; Jean Schwartz	
Honolulu Moon		
My Honolulu Lady	Lee Johnson	1898
My Honolulu Tomboy	"Sonny" Cunha	1908
My Isle of Golden Dreams	Gus Kahn; Walter Blaufuss	1919
My Little Grass Shack in Kialikahua Hawaii	Bill Cogswell; Tom Harrison; Johnny Noble	1933
My Rose of Honolulu	Tom Armstrong	1911
On the Beach at Waikiki	G. H. Stover; Henry Kailimai	1915
Sweet Hawaiian Moonlight	Harold G. Frost; F. H. Klickman	1918
They're Wearing 'em Higher in Hawaii	Joe Goodwin; Halsey K. Mohr	1917
When Those Sweet Hawaiian Babies Roll Their Eyes	Edgar Leslie; Harry Ruby	1917
Yamma Yamma Man	Otto Harback; Karl Hoschna	1908

Songs about States*

Alabamy Bound	DeSylva; Green; Henderson	1925
Alabamy Cradle Song	Kahn; Otis; Van Alstyne	1925
At a Georgia Camp Meeting	Kerry Mills	1897
At a Mississippi Cabaret	A. S. Brown; Gumble	1914
Back to Carolina You Love	Clarke; Schwartz	1914
Beneath Montana Skies	Niel Knoyle; Bill Nokes	1929
California	Jack Lait; Charlie Abot	1921
California and You	Leslie; Puck	1914
California Here I Come	Al Jolson; Bud DeSylva; Joseph Meyer	1924
Can't Get Indiana off My Mind	Robert DeLeon; Hoagy Carmichael	1940
Carolina in the Morning	Gus Kahn; Walter Donaldson	1922
Carolina Moon	Benny Davis; Joe Burke	1928
Carry Me Back to Old Virginny	James Bland	1878
Deep in the Heart of Texas	June Hershey; Don Swander	1941
Down Kentucky Way	James W. Casey	1919
Everything Is K. O. in Kentucky	Egan; Whiting	1923
Everything Is Peaches Down in Georgia	Milton Ager; George W. Meyer	1918
Florida, the Moon and You	Buck; Friml	1926
Georgia	H. Johnson; Donaldson	1922
Georgia Lullaby	Charles Cordray	1924
The Girl I Loved in Sunny Tennessee	Braisted; Carter	1899
Hello, Wisconsin	Bert Kalmar; Edgar Leslie	1917
I Want to Go Back to Michigan	Irving Berlin	1914

* In addition to these are the State College songs.

I'm Going Back to Nebraska		
In Dear Old Georgia	Williams; Van Alstyne	1905
In Dear Old Illinois	Paul Dresser	1902
In Old California With You		
In the Gold Fields of Nevada	Edgar Leslie; Archie Gottler	1915
Indiana	MacDonald; Hanley	1917
Kentucky Echoes	L. Wolfe Gilbert; Riley Reilly	1922
Louisiana Hayride	Deitz; Schwartz	1932
Louisiana Lize	Bob Cole	1899
Missouri Moon	Mitchell Parish; Henry Lodge	1929
Moonlight in Vermont	Karl Suessdorf; John Blackburn	1944
My Heart's Tonight in Texas	Roden; Witt	1900
My Louisiana Babe	C. C. Clark	1890
My Mississippi Belle	Cole; Johnson	1903
Oklahoma!	Oscar Hammerstein II; Richard Rodgers	1943
On the Oregon Trail	Billy Hill; Peter DeRose	
Roamin' to Wyomin'		
She Lives in Alabama	Edith Willard; Harry Miller	1901
She Was Bred in Old Kentucky	Braisted; Carter	1898
She's the Flower of Mississippi	Horwitz; Bowers	1901
She's the Sunshine of Virginia	MacDonald; Carroll	1916
Sleepy Hills of Tennessee	Young; Lewis; Meyer	1923
Somewhere in Old Wyoming	Mitchell Parish; Frank Perkins	1934
Stars Fell on Alabama		
Stealing to Virginia	Gus Kahn; Walter Donaldson	1923
Take Me Back to My Louisiana Home	Cobb; Edwards	1904
'Tuck Me to Sleep in My Old 'Tucky Home	Lewis; Young; Meyer	1921
Two Tickets to Georgia	C. Tobias; Coots	1933
Way Down in Ioway	Lewis; Young; Meyer	1916
We'll Have a Jubilee in My Old Kentucky Home	Coleman; Goetz; Walter Donaldson	1915
When the Moon Begins to Shine Through the Pines of Caroline	Will Hart; Ed Nelson	1918
When the Moon Shines Down on Old Alaska	Jack Frost; E. Clinton Keithly	1916
When You Dream of Old New Hampshire, I Dream of Tennessee	Jack Murphy; George L. Cobb	1916

Songs about Cities

April in Paris	E. Y. Harburg; Vernon Duke	1932
Avalon Town	Grant Clarke; Nacio Herb Brown	1928
Back, Back, Back to Baltimore	Harry Williams; Egbert Van Alstyne	1904
Bagdad	Harold Atteridge; Al Jolson	1918
Chicago	Fred Fisher	1922

Come Over to Dover	Stanley Murphy; George Botsford	1914
Constantinople	Harry Carlton; DeSylva; Brown; Henderson	1928
Dear Old Portland Town (Oregon)	Harry L. Stone	1916
Down in Dear Old New Orleans		
Goodbye Shanghai	Howard Johnson; Joseph Meyer	1921
Greenwich Village Sue	A. Swanstrom; Carey Morgan	1920
Hello 'Frisco	Jene Buck; Lou Hirsch	1915
I Want to Go to Tokyo	McCarthy; Fisher	1914
I'm Going Right Back to Chicago	Williams; Van Alstyne	1916
I'm on My Way to Mandalay	A. Bryan; Fisher	1913
It Couldn't Occur in New York	Ben Warren; Dox Cruger	1890
Little Old New York	Schwartz; Dietz	1929
London Paved With Gold	McGlennon	1892
Manhattan Serenade	Howard Johnson; Lewis Alters	1940
Moon Over Miami	Edgar Leslie; Joe Burke	1935
Nagasaki	Mort Dixon; Harry Warren	1928
On San Francisco Bay	V. Bryan; Gertrude Hoffman	1906
San Francisco	Kahn; Koper; Jurman	1936
San Francisco, the Paris of the U. S. A.	Hirshel Hendler	1912
Seattle Town	Harold Weeks	1923
Shuffle off to Buffalo	Al Dubin; Harry Warren	1932
Sidewalks of New York	Charles B. Lawler; James W. Blake	1894
Somewhere in Naples	Harry D. Kerry; J. S. Zamecnik	1921
That Tumbledown Shack in Athlone	R. W. Pasco; Monte Carlo; Alma M. Sanders	1918
Timbuctoo	Kalmar; Ruby	1920
Way Down Yonder in New Orleans	Creamer; Layton	1922
Won't You Come Over to Dover		
Ypsilanti	A. Bryan; E. Van Alstyne	1915

Songs about Rivers

Beautiful Ohio	Ballard MacDonald; Mary Earl	1918
By the Sleepy Rio Grande		
Down Around the 'Sip 'Sip 'Sippy Shore	Young; Lewis; Donaldson	1921
Moonlight on the Colorado	Billy Moll; Robert King	
Mississippi Boat Song	Frank Dumont	1891
Mississippi Mud	Harry Barris	1927
Mississippi Steamboat	Helen Walker	
On the Banks of the Wabash	Paul Dresser	1890
Swanee Butterfly	Billy Rose; Walter Donaldson	1925
Where the Dreamy Wabash Flows		

Broadway Songs

Broadway Rose	Eugene West; Martin Fried; Otis Spencer	1920
Don't Blame It All on Broadway	Joe Young; Harry Williams; Bert Grant	1913
Forty-Five Minutes From Broadway	George M. Cohan	1905
Give My Regards to Broadway	George M. Cohan	1904
Goodbye Broadway, Hello France	C. Francis Weisner; Benny Davis; Billy Baskett	1917
I'm a Vamp From East Broadway		
It's Getting Dark on Old Broadway		
It's Moonlight All the Time on Broadway	Ren Shields; Percy Wenrich	1908
On the Proper Side of Broadway on a Saturday Night	P. M.; Cobb; Gus Edwards	1902
Somewhere on Broadway	Murphy; Carroll	1917
There's a Broken Heart for Every Light on Broadway	Howard Johnson; F. Fisher	1915
When Broadway Was a Pasture	McCarthy; Pianadosi	1911

Songs about Miscellaneous Locations

Canadian Capers	Gus Chandler; Bert White; Henry Cohen	1915
Cheyenne	Harry Williams; Egbert Van Alstyne	1906
Dear Old Eastside	Gardenier; Edwards	1907
The Girl I Loved Out in the Golden West	C. H. Scoggins; Charles Avril	1903
Hindustan	Oliver G. Wallace; Harold Weeks	1918
In China	A. J. Stasney; Otto Motzan	1919
In the Heart of the Berkshire Hills	Claude Hager; Walter Goodwin	1918
It's Tulip Time in Holland	Dave Radford; Richard Whiting	1915
Norway	McCarthy; Fisher	1915
The Olympic Trail	Ray Walker; Art Smith	1934
Rocky Mountain Moon	Egan; Marshall; Whiting	1923
Russian Lullaby	Irving Berlin	1927
Siren of a Southern Sea	Abe Brashen; Harold Weeks	1921
Take Me Up to the North Pole	Halsey K. Mohr	1909
The Isle of Capri	Jimmy Kennedy; Will Grosz	1934
Underneath the Russian Moon	Kendis; Samuels; Gusman	1929
Under Western Skies	Casey; Weeks; Murtagh	1920
Way Down on Tampa Bay	A. S. Brown; Van Alstyne	1914
When It's Apple Blossom Time in Normandy	L. Wolfe Gilbert; Lewis F. Muir; Maurice Abrahams	1912
When It's Moonlight on the Alamo	A. Bryan; Fisher	1914
When It's Springtime in the Rockies	Mary Hale Woolsey; Milton Taggart; Robert Sauer	1929
Where the Lanterns Glow		

COON SONGS
(BLACKFACE)

The term "coon" applied to sheet music collecting is synonymous with the fractured English supposedly spoken by the American Black and used in the lyrics of a song. "Coon" songs, the by-product of the slavery issue, were nutured through the minstrel shows and finally evolved into a musical style gaining great status during the late Victorian age. This popularity, of course, was primarily because of the institution known as Tin Pan Alley.

The majority of song titles contained the word "coon," and the Black individual was referred to as a "coon" even by Black songwriters. It is common knowledge among Tin Pan Alley–ites that the Black composer Ernest Hogan, who wrote "All Coons Look Alike to Me," spent the remainder of his life regretting those lyrics.

In any eventuality, these songs are a part of the American heritage. So many were beautifully composed, and the songsheets were not always uncomplimentary. But with some, one must remember that the cover artists were caricature-prone, and this included the Negro as well as other ethnic groups. Any caricature is of course an exaggerated modification of an outstanding physical characteristic. To continually apologize for the word "coon" is an admission of guilt, but this guilt belongs to another age. To categorize it differently would mask the reality. The very fact that white people climbed aboard every musical innovation originated by the Blacks is a testimonial of respect. Nevertheless, there is still sensitivity to the word "coon," and it is not my intention to nourish it further. "Blackface" would be the category title most applicable to replace "Coon."

During the period from 1890 to 1910, the immensely popular coon songs fostered the breed of singers known as "coon shouters." Coon shouting was the way to plug a song and another example of the interdependence of the song and the performer. See Chapter 7 for additional information on these Coon shouters.

Coon Songs

Ain't Dat a Shame	John Queen; Walter Wilson	1901
All Coons Look Alike to Me	Ernest Hogan	1896

Back, Back, Back to Baltimore	Harry Williams; Egbert Van Alstyne	1904
Bake Dat Chicken Pie	Frank Dumont	1906
Bedelia	William Jerome; Jean Schwartz	1903
Bill Bailey, Won't You Please Come Home	Hughie Cannon	1902
Bon, Bon Buddy, the Chocolate Drop	Alex Rogers; Will Marion Cook	1907
The Coldest Coon in Town	Andrew Sterling; Harry Von Tilzer	1899
Come Back My Honey		
Coon, Coon, Coon	Jene Jefferson; Leo Friedman	1900
Darky Cavalier	David Reed, Jr.	1895
Dat's the Way to Spell Chicken	Sidney Perrin; Bob Slater	1902
De Cake Walk Queen	Harry B. Smith; Stromberg	1900
De Leader of de Company B	David Reed, Jr.	1895
Doan You Cry, Mah Honey	Albert W. Noll	1899
Don't Be What You Ain't	George V. Hobart; E. M. Royle; Silvio Hein	1905
Every Race Has a Flag But the Coon	Will A. Heelan; J. Fred Helf	1900
Ev'ry Morn I Bring Her Chicken	Harry J. Breen; T. Mayo Geary	1903
Ghost of a Coon	Williams; Walker	1900
Go Way Back and Sit Down	Al Johns	1901
Good Morning, Carrie	Cecil Mack; Albert Von Tilzer	1901
Have You Seen My Henry Brown	Dave Clark; Albert Von Tilzer	1905
Hello Ma Baby	Ida Emerson; Joe Howard	1899
Hitch on de Golden Trolley	Monroe Rosenfeld	1902
Hottest Coon in Town		
I Don't Care If You Neber Come Back	Monroe Rosenfeld	1897
I Don't Like No Cheap Man	Williams; Walker	1897
I Want dem Presents Back	West	1896
I Want Yer, Ma Honey	Fay Templeton	1895
I Wonder Why Bill Bailey Don't Come Home	Frank Fogarty; Woodward; Jerome	1902
I Wouldn't Change dat Gal for No Other	Aubrey Boucicault	1899
I'd Leave My Happy Home for You	Will A. Heelan; Harry Von Tilzer	1899
If the Man in the Moon Were a Coon	Fred Fisher	1905
I'm Going to Get Myself a Black Salome	Stanley Murphy; Ed Wynn	1908
I'se a Lady	Kennett; Udall	1899
I'se Your Nigger If You Wants Me, Liza Jane	Paul Dresser	1896
Ma' Tiger Lily	H. B. Sloane	1900
Mammy Jinny's Jubilee	Gilbert; Muir	1913
Mammy's Little Coal Black Rose	Raymond Egan; Richard Whiting	1916
Mammy's Pumpkin Colored Coon	Hillman; Perrin	1897
Mazie, My Dusky Daizy	Heelan; Helf	1901
Mr. Johnson, Turn Me Loose	Ben Harney	1896
My Baby Lize		
My Black Baby, Mine	Thomas LeMack	1896
My Coal Black Lady	W. T. Jefferson	1896

My Gal Is a High Born Lady	Barny Fagan	1896
My Hannah Lady	David Reed, Jr.	1899
My Honey Lou	Thurland Chattaway	1904
My Rainbow Coon		
New Coon in Town	Paul Allen	1883
The Phrenologist Coon	Hogan; Accooe	1901
Pliney, Come Kiss Your Baby	David Reed, Jr.	1899
Pretty Little Dinah Jones	J. S. Mullen	1902
Rastus On Parade	George Marion; Kerry Mills	1895
Roll Them Cotton Bales	J. W. Johnson; J. Rosimond Johnson	1914
Roll Dem Roly Boly Eyes	Eddie Leonard	1912
Rufus, Rastus, Jóhnson, Brown (What You (Gonna Do When de Rent Comes Round?)	Andrew Sterling; Harry Von Tilzer	1905
She's Gettin' Mo' Like the White Folks Everyday		
Since Bill Bailey Come Back Home	Billy Johnson; Seymour Furth	1902
The Sound of Chicken Frying, Dat's Music to Me	Chris Smith	1907
Sweet Emalina, My Gal	Creamer; Leighton	1917
There's a Dark Man Coming With a Bundle	Leighton Brothers	1904
Topsy	R. A. Brown	1901
Up Dar in de Sky	Davis	1892
The Warmest Baby in the Bunch	George M. Cohan	1896
The Wedding of the Chinee and the Coon	Bob Cole; Billy Johnson	1897
When It's All Goin' Out and Nothin' Comin' In	Williams; Walker	1902
When Old Bill Bailey Plays the Ukelele	Charles McCarron; Nat Vincent	1914
When Uncle Joe Plays a Rag on His Old Banjo	D. A. Esrom (Morse)	1912
When You Ain't Got No Money, Well You Needn't Come Around	Sloane; Brewster	1898
Whistling Rufus	Kerry Mills	1899
Who Dat Say Chicken in Dis Crowd	Paul Lawrence Dunbar; Will Marion Cook	1898
Who Picked the Lock on the Henhouse Door		circa 1890s
You're in the Right Church But the Wrong Pew	Cecil Mack; Chris Smith	1908
You've Been a Good Old Wagon But You Done Broke Down	Ben Harney	1896

MOTHER

It was the 1880s. Tin Pan Alley had not as yet been christened. Two distinctly different song types emanated from the Alley. The first was the rollicking, raucous, and humor-spiced Irish songs, which were the by-product of the Harrigan-Hart variety shows. The second was the morbidly sentimental "Mother" songs. She was always in her final resting place, and some loved one was forever planting, picking, or watering

74

flowers on her grave. Let's face it. One good hit deserves another, and another, and a dozen more, perhaps! The 1890s arrived and Tin Pan Alley cloaked her in an aura of long-suffering loneliness, unquestionable morality, and all the angelic attributes. This at least brought her above ground. From this period onward, hundreds of "Mother" songs were written. She has remained a very popular lady throughout the Tin Pan Alley era.

But when was the *last* "Mother" song of consequence written? The one coming quickly to my mind is "Little Old Lady," circa 1937 or thereabout. This is over thirty-five years ago! There are two plausible reasons for this truly sad state of affairs. First, it was a tired theme, having all been said so many, many times. Second, psychologically speaking, our nation of people has matured. It must have finally dawned on us that "Mother" is one of our own species, subject to all human frailties. She is sometimes divorced, smokes, drinks, and even laughs and has a good time occasionally. This, of course, leaves the lyricist little to be poetic over. In the past Tin Pan Alley has honored her, beautifully. For this we give thanks.

Mother Songs

Always Keep a Smile for Mother	Converse	1884
As I Sat Upon My Old Mother's Knee		1884
Break the News to Mother	Charles K. Harris	1897
Bringing Pretty Blossoms to Strew on Mother's Grave	T. P. Westendorf	1880
Flower From My Angel Mother's Grave	Harry Kennedy	1878
Handful of Earth From Mother's Grave	Joseph Murphy	1883
I Believe It for My Mother Told Me So	Paul Dresser	1897
I Want a Girl Just Like the Girl That Married Dear Old Dad	Will Dillon; Harry Von Tilzer	1911
I'd Be Proud to Be the Mother of a Soldier		1918
Ireland Must Be Heaven for My Mother Came From There	McCarthy; H. Johnson; Fisher	1916
Little Gray Mother	Grossman; De Costa	1915
Little Old Lady	Stanley Adams; Hoagy Carmichael	1937
Mammy Jinny's Hall of Fame	Stanley Murphy; Harry Tierney	1917
Mammy Jinny's Jubilee	Gilbert; Muir	1913
M-O-T-H-E-R	Howard Johnson; Theodore Morse	1915
Mother Is the Best Friend	J. P. Skelly	1883

Mother Machree	Rida Johnson Young; Ernest Ball	1910
Mother o'mine	Kipling; Caro Roma	
Mother of the Girl I Love	William B. Gray	1897
Mother Pin a Rose on Me	Lewis; Schlinder; Adams	1905
Mother's Last Letter to Me	C. H. Hughes	1883
A Mother's Plea for Her Son		1883
Mother's Appeal to Her Boy	J. Holmes; H. F. Smith	1889
Mother's Prayer	Arnstein; Gilbert	1932
My Mammy	Joe Young; Sam Lewis; Walter Donaldson	1921
My Mammy Lives Up in the Sky		
My Mother Was a Lady	E. B. Marks; Joe Stern	1896
My Mother's Kiss		
My Mother's Rosary	Sam M. Lewis; George W. Meyers	1915
Old Fashioned Mother	Olcott	1897
Remember Poor Mother at Home	W. A. Evans	1883
Shedding Tears o'er Mother's Grave	R. W. Rose; George A. Cragg	1883
Since Mother Passed Away	M. T. Bohannon	1893
Sing to Me Mother, Sing Me to Sleep	Callahan; Klickman	1913
Songs My Mammy Sang to Me		1894
Stick to Your Mother, Tom	E. J. Symons	1885
Stories Mother Told	Frank J. Gurney	1895
That Old Irish Mother of Mine	William Jerome; Andrew Mack	1920
There's a Mother Waiting for You at Home Sweet Home	James Thornton	1903
There's Another Picture in Mamma's Frame		
There's Nothing Will Forgive Like a Mother	Cooper; Wege Farth	1891
A Violet From My Angel Mother's Grave		1903
A Violet From Mother's Grave	Will H. Fox	1881
Why Did They Dig Ma's Grave So Deep	Joseph Skelly	1880
You Never Miss Your Mother Till She's Gone	Harry Birch	1885
You Remind Me of My Mother	George M. Cohan	1922
Your Mother Wants You Home, Boy	Paul Dresser	1904
You've Got Your Mother's Big Blue Eyes	Irving Berlin	1913

GIRLS' NAMES AND PORTRAITS

The fact that the songwriting business has been dominated by the male species undoubtedly accounts for the innumerable songs in which the title is or contains a girl's name. What name, during the Tin Pan Alley era, has been most frequently used in a song title? Your first thought, like mine, probably was "Mary." I was pleasantly surprised when I found it to be "Rose," which in my estimation is much prettier. My reasoning in regard to the popularity of "Rose" with the Alley people is as follows: Fashion is a facet of our daily lives, affecting us in many ways. Names are as fad-prone as any other commodity. When Tin Pan Alley was in full bloom, to put it facetiously, so was "Rose." The popularity of the name "Rose" during this period was heightened by its conduciveness to rhyming. Of course, "Edna" and "Gertrude" were contemporaneous with "Rose," but the lyrical potential of these names is a big goose egg! I do have a song sheet entitled "Edna," also an unlikely "Hortense."

Songs with girls' names in the title, at any point in time, reflect the attitude of the opposite sex. In the pre–1920 era were two distinct groups. The first was strictly the "love song" of male to his mate, full of adulation and yearning. The second was a "coon song" derivative ("My Tiger Lil," "Sweet Emalina, My Gal," "Mandy") humorous at times or again a love song—both with an accent.

Women's great rebellion against Victorianism came with the twenties. For the first time in history, her hair was bobbed. (At that time, it must have seemed unmercifully short!) Skirts were shockingly whacked off above the knee. Rolled-down hose and cigarette-smoking were the criteria of freedom. The sex symbol was the "vamp" (although the vamp had her beginnings prior to 1920). She could be hard-boiled or hard-hearted. "Sob Sister Sadie" was not above getting her wishes by using all her womanly wiles, including tears, leaving a path of broken-hearted men in her wake. But with all these negative attributes, she was a new and exciting creature—adoringly placed on a pedestal as usual. It is amusing to read the lyrics of these songs of the 1920s and a great insight into *this* most rebellious time.

Girls' portraits are plentiful on song sheet covers and beautifully done in many cases, such as the "Manning portraits" (see Chapter 6, Cover Artists). In addition is Albert Barbelle whose portraits are exceptional.

Songs with Girls' Names

Rose

Abie's Wild Irish Rose	Goodbye, Rose
Broadway Rose	Hard Boiled Rose
The Daughter of Rosie O'Grady	Her Name Is Rose
Down at Rosie Riley's Flat	I'll Make a Ring Around Rosie

Rose (cont'd)	Ma Blushin' Rosie	Rose of Japan
	Montmatré Rose	Rose of No Man's Land
	My Faithful Rose	Rose of the Rio Grande
	My Irish Rosie	Rose of Washington Square
	My Little Georgia Rose	Rosey, Rosey, Just Supposey
	My Little Persian Rose	Rosie My Dusky Georgia Rose
	My Southern Rose	Rosie, Sweet Rosabel
	My Wild Irish Rose	Second Hand Rose
	Pretty Rosie Kelley	Sentimental Rose
	Rose Marie	Yankee Rose
Mary	Ain't You Glad You're Home, Mary	Mary of the Prairie
	I Love the Name of Mary	Mary You're a Little Bit Old Fashioned
	Main Street Wasn't Big Enough For Mary	Mary's a Grand Old Name
	Mary	Over the Hill to Mary
	Mary Dear	Poor Little Mary
	Mary Lou	Since Mary Left the Mill
		So Long Mary
Katie	Don't Cry Katie, Dear	K-K-K-Katy
	I Wish I Could Shimmee Like My Sister Kate	Since Katie Rides a Wheel
	Katy Gray	Waitin' for Katy
		Waiting at the Gate for Katy
Sue	Coming From Church With Sue	Susie My Susie-que
	Kentucky Sue	Suzie Ma Sue
	The Meeting House Where I Met Sue	Sweet Sue
	My Greenwich Village Sue	Sweet Suzanne
	Sioux City Sue	When Susan Thompson Tries to Hit High C
	Susan	
Kitty	Kansas City Kitty	Sweet Kitty Fay
	Pretty Kitty Kelly	When Kitty and I Were Comin' Through the Rye
	Sweet Kitty Carney	
Maggie	Goodbye Maggie Doyle	Maggie the Cows Are in the Clover
	Little Maggie Monahan	Since Maggie Learned to Skate
	Maggie	When You and I Were Young Maggie
	Maggie Mooney	
	Maggie Murphy's Home	
Sally	I Wonder What's Become of Sally	Sally Ann
	My Gal Sal	Sally, Don't Dally

Marie	Goodby, Sweet Marie	Marie, Marie, Marie
	Oh Marie	Marie McGee
	Oui, Oui, Marie	When Sweet Marie Was Sweet Sixteen
	Marie	
	Marie From Sunny Italy	

Miscellaneous Names	Airy Fairy Lillian	Little Gertie Murphy
	Along Came Ruth	Little Lottie Lee
	Aunt Hannah	Louise
	Bebe	Louisiana Louise
	Bella, the Belle of Dunoon	Louisville Lou
	Bessie and Her Little Brown Bear	Lucinda I Am Waiting For You
	Betty Co-ed	Lucy Linda Lady
	Bonnie Jean	Mabel
	Chiquita	Mandy, Ain't You Comin' Out Tonight
	Cindy Lou	Mandy and Me
	Come Josephine in My Flying Machine	Marcellona
	Dear Louise	Margie
	Don't Bring Lulu	Marta
	Georgette	Martha
	Goodbye Liza Jane	Mazie
	Gretchen	Mickey
	Haidie	Mimi
	Hannah	Minnie, Shimmee for Me
	Hard Hearted Hannah	Miss Helen Hunt
	I Love the Name of Louise	Mollie-Oh
	Ida, Sweet as Apple Cider	Molly Malone
	I'm Waiting for Winnie	My Geraldine
	Iola	My Josephine
	Irene, Goodnight	My Own, Iona
	Ivy, Cling to Me	My Pearl's a Bowery Girl
	Jane	My Tiger Lily
	Jeaninne, I Dream of Lilac Time	Naomi
	Jessamine	Nay, Nay, Pauline
	Joan of Arc, I Am Calling You	No, No Nora
	Kathleen	Not Yet, Suzette
	Let's All Go 'Round to Mary Anne's	Oh Flo
	Let's All Go Up to Maud's	Oh! Helen
	Lil' Liza Jane	Oh! Mabel
	Lilac	Oh Miss Malinda
		Oh My Sweet Hortense
		Peg O' My Heart

Miscellaneous Names (cont'd)

Peggy Cline
Peggy O'Neil
Polly
Poor Pauline
Pretty Jennie Slatterly
Pretty Jessie Moore
Ramona
Rebecca
Rebecca of Sunnybrook Farm
Rosalie
Ruby, the Gem of My Heart
Sailing Down the River, Mandy and Me
Sandy
Sarah's Hat
Showing Aunt Matilda 'Round the Town

Stella
Sweet Georgia Brown
Sweet Jennie Lee
Sweet Julienne
Sweet Rosalie
Sweetheart May
Take a Day Off, Maryanne
Teresa
True Blue Lou
Virginia Lee
A Vision of Salome
When May and I Were Sweethearts Long Ago
Which Hazel
Yvette

TRANSPORTATION AND COMMUNICATION

Romance has forever been associated with transportation and communication, and romance was Tin Pan Alley's stock in trade.

Predating the Alley, steamships, boats, and railroads were the subject of many a melody, but Tin Pan Alley caused them to become legendary. Any new invention was the Alley weaver's invitation to memorialize it in song. "I'll Build a Subway to Your Heart" coincided with the building of the New York subway system. The bicycle became a national pastime in the 1890s, and songwriter Henry Dacre came forth with "Daisy Belle" ("Bicycle Built for Two"). The impact of Bell's invention on the American public was dramatic indeed, and the Alley capitalized on this with innumerable telephone songs.

The automobile, railroad, airplane, trolley, and dirigible were inspirations for countless outpourings from Tin Pan Alley. If the citizens of the United States ever had a love affair with any of these, my unqualified guess would be the railroad, for it contained one key ingredient mainly absent from all other forms of transportation. This is the hypnotic rhythm (an innate need of humans) of the train's engine superimposed on the clickety clack cadence of wheels against track. I don't in the slightest degree mean to discount the automobile. We are geared to the wheel and have been for quite some time now. Auto associated songs are high, if not near, the top of the song sheet wanted list.

Two other forms of transportation and communication should be cited here. Now that walking has been established as *the* most beneficial exercise, the collecting of the many song sheets dealing with this most primitive form of locomotion would be popular. "Walking My Baby Back Home," "Let's Take an Old-Fashioned Walk," "Let's Take a Walk Around the Block" are some examples.

The other is the United States mail. To illustrate how intertwined one industry becomes with another, consider the postcard, which incidentaly was born about the same time as Tin Pan Alley and was also highly successful. In 1908 the Alley published "The Post Card Girl" in song, and a leather postcard (collection of the author) from 1911 shows an upright piano with two embracing lovers perched thereon. The caption reads "Try this on your piano," which was a stock phrase used on nearly all sheet music to advertise the latest song issues.

Many songs dealing with letters or the United States Postal Department are available. These include songs about mail carriers and stamps. The song sheet lends itself well to the collecting of anything to do with transportation and communication. Plentiful, they are not, but in sufficient quantity to make the search worthwhile.

Songs about Transportation and Communication

Casey Jones
The Chicago Express
De Gospel Train
Eastern Train
The Elevated Railroad
Honeymoon Express
I'm Going to Take the Train For Home Sweet Home
Meet Me at the Station, Dear
My Dad's the Engineer
My Dream Train
Oh! Mister Railroad Man

The Railroad (cont'd)	Oh, My Railroad Man
	On the Five-Fifteen
	Pullman Porters on Parade
	Railroad Jim
	Red Ball Express
	Shuffle Off to Buffalo
	That Railroad Rag
	There's a Lot of Stations on My Railroad Track
	The Train Rolled on
	Two Tickets to Georgia
	Wabash Cannonball
	When the Midnight Choo-Choo Leaves for Alabam'
	You Once Were Excess Baggage, Now You're Only Common Freight
The Automobile	Big Red Motor and Little Blue Limousine
	Black Maria
	Gasoline Gus and His Jitney Bus
	He'd Have to Get Under—Get Out and Get Under His Automobile
	Henry's Made a Lady out of Lizzie
	Hunkatin'
	I'm Wild About Horns on Automobiles That Go Ta-Ta-Ta-Ta
	The Jaunting Car (Auto?)
	Keep Away From the Fellow Who Owns an Automobile
	The Lady Chauffeur
	The Little Old Ford Rambled Right Along
	The Low Backed Car (Auto)
	The Motor King March
	My Auto Show Girl
	My Merry Oldsmobile
	On an Automobile Honeymoon, Ham Tree
	The Pace That Kills
	The Packard and the Ford
	The Six Cylinder Kid
	Take Me 'Round in a Taxicab
	Toot Your Horn, Kid, You're in a Fog
	Would You Like to Motor With Me Mater
Steamboat	Fire Ship
	The Good Ship Maryann
	Here Comes the Showboat
	My Mariucci Take a Steamboat
	Oceana Roll
	On the Mississippi
	On the Old Fall River Line

Steamboat (cont'd)	Sailing Away on the Henry Clay
	Sailing Down the Chesapeake Bay
	See Those Mississippi Steamboats on Parade
	Steamboat Bill
	Steamboat Rag
	Waitin' for the Robert E. Lee
	The Wreck of the Titanic

Telephone and Telegraph	All Alone (Irving Berlin)
	All Alone (Harry Von Tilzer)
	Call Me Up Some Rainy Afternoon
	Central, Give Me Back My Dime
	Hello Central Give Me Heaven
	Hello, Central, Hello
	I Guess I'll Have to Telegraph My Baby
	I Just Received a Telegraph From Baby
	If You're Lonesome, Just Telephone Me
	Kissing Papa Through the Telephone
	The Telephone Girl
	Telephone Me, Baby

United States Postal Department	The Faded Letter
	I'm Going to Write You a Letter
	I'm Gonna Sit Right Down and Write Myself a Letter
	The Letter Edged in Black
	The Letter That Never Came
	Loveletters in the Sand
	My Post Card Girl
	Parcel Post March and Two Step
	Waiting for the Evening Mail

Airborne Transportation	Aeroplane Dip (Hesitation)
	The Airplane Waltz
	The Cloud Kisser (Rag)
	Come Josephine in My Flying Machine
	Come Take a Trip in My Airship
	Goin' Up
	Take Me Up in Your Airship, Willie
	Take Me Up With You, Dearie
	Up, Up, Up in My Aeroplane
	Wait'll You Get Them Up in the Air, Boys

Walking	Hike to the Pike
	If You'll Walk With Me
	Let's Take a Walk Around the Block

83

Walking (cont'd)	Let's Take an Old Fashioned Walk
	Walking My Baby Back Home
Miscellaneous	Bicycle Built for Two
	Courtin' on a Wheel
	Covered Wagon Days
	Jimmy the Pride of Newspaper Row
	On a Good Old Time Sleighride
	On a Good Old Trolley Ride
	Rolling in His Little Rolling Chair
	She Reads the New York Papers Everyday
	Since Katy Rides a Wheel
	Thanks For the Buggie Ride
	Trolley Car Swing
	Trolley Song
	Why Don't You Try the Rolling Chair Song
	You'll Have to Transfer

CURRENT EVENTS

Love is the never-ending and enduring musical theme. Fashion, food, dances, rhythms, transportation, wars, and beverages are also enduring but subject to change and vogue. Current events are something else again. They are a comet Kahoutek. For one fleeting and gloriously flaming moment, they occupy the minds of the populace. Whether catastrophic, political, or dedicatory in context, their respective headlines were an injection of adrenaline into the Alley. Competition was keen here; more rumor was sufficient to set the song weavers into a fever of creativity.

Tin Pan Alley can by no means be given credit for the political theme song. Popular songs were political in nature long before Monroe Rosenfeld gave the Alley its famous name. Campaigns had been launched with a song; laws had been enacted through the help of a song. But the ingenuous Tin Pan Alley showed how it should *properly* be done. Inaugerals, dedications, expositions, and catastrophes were waltzed, marched, polka-ed, and sung to whatever tune the Alley deemed fitting to the occasion.

Under the current events category one can choose to collect political, expositions, catastrophes, famous news celebrities, news songs, or dedications.

Dedications should be divided into two separate classifications. The first would consist of dedications to famous news celebrities, for example, "The Ship Named U. S. A.," which was dedicated to Woodrow Wilson, ties in with news or current happenings. The other category is show people dedications and has nothing to do with current events. This classification might more appropriately be placed alongside movie or stage stars (see Chapter 7). I think, however, the grouping of all dedications under one heading would prove less confusing.

It was normal practice for songwriters to dedicate a song to someone associated with it, perhaps the singer who plugged it or the star of the movie having this particular composition as its theme. The singing and movie idols of the day were the subject of many dedications by the songwriters. This practice served a triple purpose. First, the connection of a hit song with a singing or movie star was excellent advertising. Second, a photograph of the star usually appeared on the song sheet cover and was great exposure for the star. Third, it served as a gesture of friendship and admiration or a thank you. The phrase "This song is respectfully dedicated to . . ." was usually placed near the top border of the song sheet cover. It may also appear elsewhere on the cover or inside on the title page. It is easily overlooked, so keep your eyes wide open.

Political Songs

Blaine, Blaine, Blaine of Maine
Blaine for President
Four More Years in the White House (Tribute to Wilson's Wedding)
General Pershing
Goodbye Teddy Roosevelt
Hurrah for Blaine and Logan
Marshall Haig
President Garfield's Funeral March
The Road Is Open Again (Franklin D. Roosevelt)
That Ragtime Suffragette
Taft March
Wilson That's All
The Woodrow Wilson March and Twostep

Expositions—(Festivals, Trade fairs, Roundups)	After the Ball (Advertised as "The Only Recognized World's Fair Song" 1893)
	After the Fair (1893 World's Fair)
	At the Hippodrome (1925 Atlantic and Pacific Highways and Electricity Exposition, Portland, Oregon)
	The Cascades—a Rag (St. Louis World's Fair 1904)
	Father of the Land We Love (Two-Hundredth Birthday of George Washington 1931)
	Glory of Jamestown (1907 Jamestown Tercentenary Exposition)
	The Greater Seattle March and Two Step (1909 Alaska-Yukon-Pacific Exposition)
	Lewis and Clark Exposition March (1905 Portland, Oregon)
	Meet Me in St. Louis, Louis (1904 World's Fair)
	My Heart Goes Back to Dear Old Pendleton (Official Song of Pendleton, Oregon Roundup 1914)
	The Official Souvenir of the Pageant and Masque (Louisiana Territory 1914)
	The Paystreak (Alaska-Yukon-Pacific Exposition 1909)
	San-Fran-Pan March (San Francisco Exposition 1915)
	Seattle Exposition March (1909 Alaska-Yukon-Pacific Exposition)
	The Streets of Cairo (1904 Salute to the St. Louis World's Fair)
News Songs	I'll Dig a Subway to Your Heart (New York Subway Construction 1914)
	Lindberg, the Eagle of the U. S. A. (1927)
	The Little Newsboy's Death (1898 Eleven-year-old newsboy struck by cable car)
	Lucky Lindy (1927 Transatlantic Flight)
	Panama Canal March and Two Step (1914)
	Perry's Victory (1913 Raising of His Flagship *Niagara*)
	Salute to the Panama Canal (1914)
	They Can't Make a Monkey out of Me (Scope's Monkey Trial)
	Triumphant Lindberg March and Fox Trot (1927)
	Who'll Take the Place of the Songbird Now Gone (Caruso's Death 1923)
Catastrophes	The Bank Has Failed Today (1890)
	The Johnstown Flood (1889)
	The Sweetheart That I Lost in Dear Old Frisco (1906 Earthquake)
	The Wreck of the Titanic (1912)
News Dedications	Dope-Rag (Dedicated to Loyal Order of Moose 1910)
	Hello Bill (1907 To the Elk's Club)

New Dedications (cont'd)   I'm in Love With a Mystic Shriner (To Ancient Arabic Order of
                                 the Mystic Shrine 1920)
                             Moose Rag (Dedicated to Loyal Order of Moose 1910)
                             An Orchid to You (To Walter Winchell 1933)
                             Seattle (To Famous War Chief Seattle 1909)
                             The Ship Named U. S. A. (To President Wilson)
                             Siamese Patrol (To Tschielalongkorn—King of Siam 1902)

Star Dedications   Allah (Mme. Alla Nazimova 1920)
                             Daddy Long Legs (Ruth Chatterton 1914)
                             Little Colonel (Shirley Temple 1935)
                             Love Sings a Song in My Heart (To Laura LaPlant 1928)
                             Mae Marsh Waltzes (Mae Marsh)
                             Mandalay (To Abe Lyman 1924)
                             Mickey (Mabel Normand 1918)
                             Oh Helen! (Fatty Arbuckle 1918)
                             Peg O' My Heart (Laurette Taylor 1913)
                             Ramona (Dolores Del Rio 1927)
                             Sipping Cider Thru' a Straw (Fatty Arbuckle 1919)
                             Stung (To All the Little Teddy Bears 1908)
                             Tears (Norma Tamadge 1918)
                             When You're a Long, Long Way From Home (Bessie Wynn 1914)
                             Who Paid the Rent for Mrs. Rip Van Winkle (Ed Morton 1914)

CHILDREN

Tin Pan Alley never truly gave children their just dues in the popular song. Other than the tear-jerkers, school songs, and the Mammy lullabies (croons), they seemed at a loss as to what to write about. But, after all, the Alley was nothing more or less than a reflection of its customers, and the customers were the people.

The wish to escape responsibility, occasionally, is natural to all of us. It is pure speculation that children, being overly abundant in supply, served only to remind parents of the many mouths to feed.

In any eventuality, whatever inspired Tin Pan Alley to create the Mammy lullabies or croons, the end result was a group of heartrending melodies with exquisitely tender lyrics. Their quality completely made up for lack in quantity. The song sheet covers tug at your heart strings, and the titles are nothing less than beautiful. The tear-jerkers told tearful tales, but the Mammy lullabies spoke softly of love.

Introducing the Song Sheet

Although these songs have been referred to in the following manner—Mammy lullabies, Mammy croons, Negro lullabies, coon croons—the Mammy lullaby is most apt, since *Mammy* was nearly always a part of the title, and lullabies they were. Although the word *croon* was not used exclusively in connection with lullabies, my contention is that the Mammy lullabies will eventually be referred to as merely "croons."

The most famous and best loved children song was neither a *tear-jerker* nor a croon but a happy, reminiscing song. Gus Edwards' "School Days" captures this honor.

Mammy Lullabies (Croons)

Hush Little Baby, Don't You Cry	Rosenfeld	1884
Hushaby Ma Baby (Missouri Waltz)	Logan	1914
If Every Star Was a Pickaninny	Joe McCarthy; Leo Edwards	
Little Alabama Coon	Hattie Starr	1893
Little Puff of Smoke, Goodnight	White; Lardner	1909
Ma Little Sunflower Goodnight	Weslyn; Vanderpool	1919
Mammy's Kinky Headed Coon	Harry Von Tilzer	1899
Mammy's 'Lasus Candy Child	Mack; Cook	1909
Mammy's Little Black Faced Child		
Mammy's Little Coal Black Rose	Raymond Egan; Richard Whiting	1916
Mammy's Little Pickaninny Boy	Williams; Walker	1896
Mammy's Little Pumpkin Colored Coon	Hillman; Perrin	1897
Mammy's Little Silver Lining		
Mammy's Little Sunny, Honey Boy		
My Sugar Coated Chocolate Boy		
Only a Little Yaller Coon		
Sandman is a Comin' fo' Ma Baby		
When Mammy Puts Her Pickaninny Boy to Bed		
You's Honey to Your Mammy Just the Same		

Others

Abie, the Sporty Kid		
After School		
All Aboard For Blanket Bay	Andrew Sterling; Harry Von Tilzer	1910
The Babies on Our Block	Ed Harrigan; David Braham	1879
Baby Shoes	Joe Goodwin; Ed Rose	1916
Baby's Laughing in Her Sleep	Gussie L. Davis	1892
Baby's Lullaby		
Baby's Prayer	R. C. Halle	1898
Bundle of Joy		

Childhood Joys	Adelaide K. Mills	1912
Cradle Song	Henry J. Sayers; Frank Howard	1883
Dear Little Boy of Mine	Brennan; Ball	1918
Fly Away, Birdie, to Heaven		
For Sale—a Baby	Charles K. Harris	1903
Guess How Much the Baby Weighs	unknown	1884
How Much Does the Baby Weigh	Will S. Hayes	1880
The Humpty Dumpty Kid	Hamill; Wenrich	1908
I Ain't Seen No Messenger Boy	Nathen Bivens	1899
I Don't Want to Play in Your Yard	Philip Wingate; H. W. Petrie	1894
I Faw Down and Go Boom	Jasper Brockman; Leonard Stevens; B. B. B.	1928
I Won't Play With You		
I'm Just a Lonely Little Kid	Jack Norworth; Al Piantadosi	1922
I'm Tying the Leaves So They Won't Come Down	E. S. S. Huntington; J. F. Helf	1907
In the House of Too Much Trouble	Will A. Heelan; J. Fred Helf	1900
Jimmy, the Pride of Newsboy Row	A. Baldwin Sloane	1900
Just a Baby's Prayer at Twilight	Sam Lewis; Joe Young; M. K. Jerome	1918
Just For the Sake of Our Daughter	Monroe Rosenfeld	1897
Kid Days	Jesse Glick; Irvin Wilson	1919
The Kid in the Three Cornered Pants	Al Lewis; J. J. Loeb	1937
Little Boy Blue	Ethelbert Nevin	1891
Little Boy Called Taps	Madden; Morse	1904
Little Daughter Nell	Harrigan; Braham	1893
Little Empty Stockings	Harry Kennedy	1883
Little Johnny Dugan	LeMack; Mack	1893
Little Lost Child	Ed Marks; Joe Stern	1894
Little Man You've Had a Busy Day	Maurice Sigler; Al Hoffman; Mabel Wayne	1934
Looking for a Little Boy	Bolton; Thompson; Ira Gershwin; George Gershwin	1925
Lullaby Land	Frank Davis; M. Prival	1919
Mr. Radio Man	Schuster; White; Friend	1924
Nobody's Little Girl	Drislane; Morse	1907
Olcott's Lullaby	Chauncey Olcott	1899
Only Me	Ford; Bratton	1894
Pat For Your Baby	Aubrey Boucicault	1898
The Picture of My Baby on the Wall		
Stay in Your Own Back Yard	Kennett; Udall	1899
Playmates	Burke; Monaco	1940
Put My Little Shoes Away	Mitchell; Pratt	1873
Rags	Silver; Fain; Richman	1926
Rockaby Baby	Effie I. Canning	1885

School Days	Cobb; Edwards	1907
She's the Image of Her Mother		
Sleep, Baby, Sleep	John J. Handley	1885
Sonny Boy	DeSylva; Brown; Henderson	1928
Ten Little Fingers and Ten Little Toes	Ira Shuster; Ed G. Nelson	1921
There's No More Buster Brown	Harry Breen; James Conlin	1908
They Always Pick on Me	Murphy; Von Tilzer	1911
Toyland	Glen MacDonough; Victor Herbert	1903
Two Dirty Little Hands	Cobb; Edwards	1906
Two Little Baby Shoes	Madden; Morse	1907
Two Little Girls in Blue	Charles Graham	1893
Two Little Ragged Urchins	Frank Howard	1885
Won't You Come and Play With Me		1896

FLORA, FAUNA, AND OTHER EARTH CREATURES

Now that so many of our Earth creatures are on the endangered species list, and increased interest regarding the coinhabitants of our world is evident, flora and fauna song sheets would prove popular.

The *rose* is symbolic of *love,* which in turn is the basic ingredient of the popular song. Like the name Rose, it surpasses all other flower-related songs. The Rose songs are monotonously repetitious; they exceed other flowers by 20 to 1. Daisies and violets are the two runners-up. A veritable garden of flowers can be yours with the song sheet covers. Especially attractive are the linens (Chapter 7). These were more often than not floral in composition.

The dance craze consisted of dance steps associated with the animal kingdom. This is the best source for animal associated song sheets. The grizzly bear, fox trot, bunny hug, kangaroo hop, and tiger rag are a few examples. There are many more.

Flora

After They Gather the Hay	Jasper J. Walker; Janet Allen	1906
And the Green Grass Grew All Around	William Jerome; Henry Von Tilzer	1912
Blue Bell	Madden; Morse	1904
Blue Grass Echos		
Cherry Blossoms	Emma I. Hart	1907
Cherry Song		
Daisies Won't Tell	Anita Owens	1908
Dance of the Goldenrods		
Down Among the Sugar Cane	Cecil Mack; Chris Smith	1908

Down By the Old Apple Tree	Wilson; Brennan	1923
Down in the Old Cherry Orchard		
Down Where the Cotton Blossoms Grow	Sterling; Von Tilzer	1901
Dublin Daisies		
Easter Lillies		
Gathering the Myrtle With Mary	William J. Scanlan	1886
Golden Hearted Daisies		
Honeysuckle and the Bee	Albert H. Fitz; William H. Penn	1901
I'll Be With You in Apple Blossom Time	Fleeson; Albert Von Tilzer	1920
I'll Be With You in Honeysuckle Time		
In the Orange Blossom Land		
In the Shade of the Old Apple Tree	Harry Williams; Egbert Van Alstyne	1905
It's Lilac Time in Lover's Lane		
Jeaninne I Dream of Lilac Time	L. Wolfe Gilbert; Nathaniel Shillkret	1928
Just a Chain of Daisies	Anita Owen	1911
Little Bunch of Shamrocks	William Jerome; Harry Von Tilzer	1913
Love Me Like the Ivy Loves the Old Oak Tree	George J. Moriarty; Richard Whiting	1914
Message of the Violet	Pixley; Luders	1902
Mid the Orange Trees and Blossoms She Is Waiting	Robert T. Skilling	1901
Narcissus	Nevin	1891
Only a Pansy Blossom	Eben Rexford; Frank Howard	1883
Shade of the Sheltering Palms	Leslie Stuart	1900
Somewhere in France Is the Lily	Howard; Clark; Johnson	1917
Strawberries		
Sweet Bunch of Lilacs	Charles A. Gardner	
Three Leaves of Shamrock	James McGuire	1889
Tiptoe Through the Tulips	Al Dubin; Joe Burke	1929
Under the Bamboo Tree	Bob Cole; Billy Johnson	1902
Under the Old Oak Tree		
Underneath the Weeping Willow Tree		
Violets	Julian Fane; Ellen Wright	1900
Voice of the Violet		
Wedding of the Lily and the Rose	Thomas LeMack; Andrew Mack	1892
When a Peach From Georgia Weds a Rose From Alabam'		
When It's Peach Pickin' Time in Georgia		
When the Autumn Leaves are Turning Gold		
When the Bloom Is on the Heather		
When the Daisies Bloom		
When the Trees Shed Their Leaves in the Fall		
Where the Black Eyed Susans Grow	David Radford; Richard Whiting	1917
Where the Morning Glories Twined Around the Door	Harry Von Tilzer	1905

Where the Sweet Magnolias Grow	Sterling; Von Tilzer	1886
You Mustn't Pick Plums From My Plum Tree	A. J. Lamb; Albert Von Tilzer	1904
You Won't Have to Pick Any Daisies		
You're the Fairest Little Daisy		
You're the Sweetest Bunch of Violets		

Roses

Faded Rose		
The Fatal Rose of Red	Gardenier; Helf	1900
For You a Rose	Cobb; Edwards	1917
Garden of Roses	Dempsey; Schmidt	1909
Garland of Old Fashioned Roses	Musgrove; Keithly	1911
Here's to the Rose	H. Sylvester Krouse	1899
If You Were the Opening Rose		
Love Among the Roses	Delahanty; Coffin	1869
Love Sends a Little Gift of Roses	Cooke; Openshaw	1919
Mammy's Little Coal Black Rose	Raymond Egan; Richard Whiting	1916
Mighty Lak' a Rose	Ethelbert Nevin	1901
Moonlight and Roses	Ben Black; Neil Moret	1925
Mother Pin a Rose on Me	Lewis; Schlinder; Adams	1905
My Pretty Red Rose	J. P. Skelly	1877
Only a Rose	Brian Hooker; Rudolph Friml	1925
Only a Rosebud	Cara Roma	1895
Red, Red, Rose	Rogers; Cook	1908
Roses Bloom for Lovers	Granichstaedten	1912
Roses Bring Dreams of You	Herbert Ingraham	1908
Roses of Picardy	Weatherly; Wood	1916
When the Twilight Came to Kiss the Rose Goodnight	Roden; Petrie	1912
When You Wore a Tulip and I Wore a Big Red Rose	Jack Mahoney; Percy Wenrich	1914

Fauna

Bessie and Her Little Brown Bear	Jack Norworth; A. Von Tilzer	1906
Buffalo Rag	Tom Turpin	1904
The Cats Have Gone Away		
Cat's Whiskers	Fred Tibbot; George Rex	1923
The Eagle and the Lion		
The Fox Hunters' March	William H. Penn	1900
Horsie Keep Your Tail Up		
Kill That Bear		
The Kitty and the Owl		
Monkey Rag	Chris Smith	1911

Old Yeller Dog of Mine
Possum and Sweet Potato
Preacher and the Bear   Arthur Longbrake   1904
They Gotta Quit Kicking My Dawg Around   Webb M. Oungst; Cy Perkins   1912
Two Little Kittens
What Does the Cat Mean When He Says Meow?   Pease; Granlund; Nelson   1924
What D'ye Mean You Lost Your Dog?   Thomas S. Allen; Jos. N. Daly   1913
When Hector Was a Pup
Who's Afraid of the Big Bad Wolf?   Frank E. Churchill; Ann Ronell 1933

Other Earth Creatures

Be My Little Baby Bumblebee   Stanley Murphy; H. T. Marshall 1912
Bees Knees   Wood; Leslie; Lopez   1923
Bird on Nellie's Hat   Arthur Lamb; Alfred Solmon   1906
Blue Bird   Earl Carroll; Al Piantadosi   1916
Bob White What You Gonna Sing Tonight   Johnny Mercer; Bernie Hanighen 1937
Bye Bye Blackbird   Mort Dixon; Ray Henderson   1926
Chanticleer Rag
The Eagle and the Lion
The Froggies Lullaby
Hen on the Nest
In the Valley Where the Bluebirds Sing   Rosenfeld; Solman   1902
The Kitty and the Owl
Let's All Sing Like the Birdies Sing   Hargreaves; Damerell; Evans   1923
The Moth and the Flame   George Taggart; Max S. Witt   1898
My Skylark Love
Poor Butterfly   John Golden; Ray Hubbell   1916
Poor Little Butterfly
Tale of the Bumblebee
Two Little Lovebirds
When Bob White Is Whistling in the Meadow   Monroe Rosenfeld   1906
When the Bees are in the Hive
When the Mocking Birds Are Singing in the   Lamb; Blake   1905
    Wildwood
When the Red Red Robin Goes Bob Bob   Harry Woods   1926
    Bobbin' Along
When the Robins Nest Again   Frank Howard   1883
Where the Chicken Got the Axe   Will H. Mayo; William Glenroy   1893
Where the Sparrows and Chippies Parade   Harrigan; Braham   1888
Wise Old Owl

NOVELTY OR   In the true sense of the term, sentimentality was Tin Pan
COMICAL SONGS   Alley's meat and potatoes. Novelty and comical songs, meta-

phorically speaking, were the spicy fare that livened up an otherwise monotonous diet.

Although coon songs were most often comical in nature, they are a distinct classification in themselves. Irish songs of the 1880s (Harrigan and Hart) and later, also humorous in the majority of cases, fall into their own category, Irish songs.

Not until the twenties and thirties did the song spinners fully develop the novelty song potential. As always with Tin Pan Alley products, novelty songs were a musical diary of the time. The appetite for this type of song seemed insatiable. Quite often, as in "It Ain't Gonna Rain No Mo'," a dozen or two extra verses were included. One song boasts forty-four additional verses.

Novelty Songs

Barnacle Bill the Sailor	C. Robinson and F. Luther	1920
Barney Google	Billy Rose and C. Conrad	1923
Bees Knees	Wood, Leslie, and Lopez	1923
The Bum Song	McClintock	1928
Cat's Whiskers	Tibbot and Rex	1923
Chili Bean	Brown and Albert Von Tilzer	1920
Dancin' Dan	Tracey and Stanley	1923
Down By the Winegar Woiks	Bestor, Lewis, and Donovan	1925
Go Long Mule	Creamer and King	1924
Goofus	Kahn, King, and Harold	1930
The Grass is Always Greener	Egan and Whiting	1924
Hallalujah I'm a Bum	Version and arrangements (Jack Waite)	1928
He Used to Be a Farmer But He's A Big Town Slicker Now	Sterling and Harry Von Tilzer	1919
The Hoodoo Man	Nacio Herb Brown	1924
Horses	Whiting and Gay	1926
How Do You Do Everybody	Fleming, Harrison, and DeVell	1924
I Faw Down and Go Boom	Brockman, Stevens, and B.B.B.	1928
I Walked Back from the Buggy Ride	Adono, Curtsinger, and Bibo	1927
I'm Gonna Dance Wit de Guy Dat Brung Me	O'Keefe and Archer	1927
It Ain't Gonna Rain No Mo'	Wendell Hall	1923
Last Night on the Back Porch	Brown and Schraubstader	1923
The Little Wooden Whistle Wouldn't Whistle	Von Tilzer and Curtis	1923
Mr. Gallagher and Mr. Shean	Gallagher and Shean	1922

Mr. Radio Man	Schuster, White, and Friend	1924
The Mummies Ball	Gunsky and Goldstein	1921
My Old Man	Dixon and Woods	1929
Nobody Else Can Love Me Like My Old Tomato Can	Downs and Baskette	1923
Oh, How I Love My Darling	Leslie and Woods	1924
Oh, How She Lied	White and Will Donaldson	1923
Red Hot Mamma	Wells, Cooper, and Rose	1924
Red Nose Pete	Freedman and Link	1924
Runnin' Wild	Grey, Wood, and Gibbs	1922
Salt Your Sugar	Simons	1923
Seven-eleven or My Dixie Pair o' Dice	Brown and Walter Donaldson	1923
She Was Just a Sailor's Sweatheart	Joe Burke	1925
Show Me the Way to Go Home	Irving King	1925
The Sneak	Nacio Herb Brown	1922
Thanks for the Buggy Ride	Jules Bufford	1925
To the Steins	Doyle	1930
True Blue Sam	Brown and Walter Donaldson	1922
Waltz Recipe	Weder, Nathan, and Rosenblum	1932
Wanted a Pal By the Name of Mary	Miller	1925
Weegee, Weegee Tell Me Do	Jerome and Harry Von Tilzer	
Yes, We Have No Bananas	Silver and Cohn	1923

SPORTS AND GAMES

If scarcity dictates price, the sport-associated song sheet would be the top money-maker. We are a sports-oriented nation. Be it participant or observer, an important slice of our national recreational time is consumed by these activities. The forty-hour work week has surely played an important role in the development of the sports industry by giving the average man or woman more free time.

Comparatively speaking, there were few sports-associated songs. Seeming to top the list of these tune types are horse racing and polo. If one included college fight songs, the list would lengthen considerably, for they are related to football. I do think, though, they should be properly placed in a distinct category of college songs.

Games follow the pattern of sports and are in even scarcer supply. Methinks the game of love holds a greater fascination. Tin Pan Alley—ites thought so too, and it appears they were right!

Sports

A Hunting We Will Go		1883
Cup Hunters	Julius Lenzberg	1915
Finnegan, the Umpire	Monroe Rosenfeld	1890
The Fox Hunters' March	William H. Penn	1900
The Gay Golf Girl		
The Gliders-Skating Waltz	William Schroeder	1916
Horses	Richard Whiting; Byron Gay	1926
The Hunt Club	Theodore O. Taubert	1915
I Wonder Where My Easy Rider's Gone	Shelton Brooks	1913
I've Gone Goofy Over Miniature Golf	Leon Diston; Mitchell Parish; Frank Perkins	1925
The Lion Hunter's Waltzes	Clyde L. Craig	1901
One-a-Strike	Arthur Longbrake	1908
The Ragtime Jockey Man	Irving Berlin	1912
The Steeple Chase	Harry J. Lincoln	1914
Take Me Out to the Ball Game	Jack Norworth; Albert Von Tilzer	1908
Take Your Girl to the Ball Game	Cohan; Jerome; Schwartz	1908
The Umpire is a Most Unhappy Fellow		

Games

Checkers	Edgar Allen; Leo Edwards	1919
Crossword Mama, You Puzzle Me	Clare; Raskin; Monaco	1924
A Pack of Cards	Henry Reilly	1892
Seben Come, Eleben Rag	W. J. Bay	1899
Seven or Eleven (My Dixie Pair-O-Dice)	Lew Brown; Walter Donaldson	1923
Since Ma Is Playing Mah Jong		
Weegee, Weegee (Tell Me Do)	William Jerome; Harry Von Tilzer	1920

CONFLICTS

The Illusion of War

By Richard Legallienne

War I do abhor, and yet how sweet
The sound along the marching street
Of Drum and Fife, and the whole
Dark butchering without a soul
Without a soul—save this bright treat
Of heady music, sweet as Hell.
And even my peace abiding feet
Go Marching with the marching street,
For yonder goes the fife,
And what care I for human life!

The tears fill my astonished eyes,
And my full heart is like to break.
And yet it is embannered lies,
A dream those drummers make
Oh, it is wickedness to clothe
Yon hideous, grinning thing that stalks
Hidden in music like a queen
That in a garden of glory walks
'Till good men love the thing they loathe,
Art, thou has many infamies,
But not an infamy like this
Oh, snap the fife and still the drum
And show the monster as she is.

This poem, "Illusion of War" by Richard Legallienne, speaks mightily of the powerful and hypnotic influence music plays in association with wars. Whether beneficially or destructively, and the war category sadly enough embraces the latter, music moves the emotions like no other art form.

It is not possible to write of Tin Pan Alley without mentioning its ancestry. Songs written at the time of our country's infancy were religious, political, or patriotic in essence. The Civil War inspired the writing of a great number of patriotic songs. The years of the Spanish American war, since they were of short duration, produced few songs. I suppose by the time songwriters got in the mood to write, it was all over.

World War I came, and the song smiths were ready with piano and pen to set every sentiment to music. Emotions ran rampant, from "Don't Take My Darling Boy Away" to "America, Here's My Boy," depending on the national political view of the moment. The songs were comical, tragic, and highly patriotic. 'Twas during this war that, to save paper, the old large sized song sheet gave way to the present standard size. Thus it remains. During the war period, songs were printed in four sizes—large, standard, small, and miniature for the armed forces. The miniatures are obviously quite scarce since that in my collection is the only one known to me.

Of the hundreds of songs published during the First World War, "Over There" by George M. Cohan was by far the most popular. Although issued under three different covers, Norman Rockwell's dramatic portrayal of soldiers singing by a camp-fire is the most desirable and hard to come by.

War Songs

America Here's My Boy	Sterling and Lange	1917
Au Revoir, But Not Goodbye	Brown and Albert Von Tilzer	1917
Bing! Bang! Bing 'em on the Rhine	Mahoney and Flynn	1918
Don't Cry Frenchie, Don't Cry	Lewis, Young, and Donaldson	1919
Dreaming of Home Sweet Home	MacDonald and Hanely	1918
Gee! What a Wonderful Time We'll Have When the Boys Come Home	Mary Earl	1917
Good-by Ma, Good-by Pa	Herschell and Walker	1918
Goodbye Broadway, Hello, France	Reisner, Davis, and Baskette	1917
Hello, Central, Give Me No Man's Land	Lewis, Young, and Schwartz	1918
Hinkey-Dinkey Parlez-Vous (Copyrighted in 1924)	Anonymous—Dubin, Mills, McHugh, and Dash	1918
How 'ya Gonna Keep 'em Down on the Farm	Young, Lewis, and Walter Donaldson	1919
I Don't Want to Get Well	Pease and Johnson	1917
I Love Her (Ooh La La La)	Porter	1918
I'd Like To See the Kaiser With a Lily in His Hand	Leslie, Johnson, and Frisch	1918
If He Can Fight Like He Can Love Goodnight Germany	Clarke, Howard, and Meyer	1918
I'm Hitting the Trail to Normandy	Charles Snyder	1917
Joan of Arc, They Are Calling You	Bryan, Weston, and Wells	1917
Just a Baby's Prayer at Twilight	Lewis, Young, and Jerome	1918
Just Like Washington Crossed the Delaware, General Pershing Will Cross the Rhine	Johnson and Meyer	1918
Liberty Bell, It's Time to Ring Again	Goodman and Mohr	1917
Lorraine My Beautiful Alsace Lorraine	Bryan and Fisher	1917
Mammy's Chocolate Soldier	Mitchell and Gottler	1918
My Barney Lies Over the Ocean—Just Like He Lied to Me	Lewis, Young, and Donaldson	1919
My Belgian Rose	Benoit, Levenson, and Gaston	1918
My Uncle Sammy Gals	Frost and Klickmann	1918
Oh Frenchy!	Erlich and Conrad	1918
Oh! How I Hate to Get Up in the Morning	Berlin	1918
Our Lanky Yankee Boys in Brown	Madden, Roden, and Morse	1917
Over There	George M. Cohan	1918
The Rose of No Man's Land	Caddigan and Brennan	1918
Roses of Lorraine	Carter and Smith	1918
There's a Little Blue Star in the Window	Armstrong and Klickmann	1918

They Were All Out of Step But Jim	Berlin	1918
Tip-Top Tipperary Mary	MacDonald and Carrol	1914
We Don't Want the Bacon—What We Want Is a Piece of the Rhine	Carr, Russell, and Havens	1918
We'll Knock the Heligo—into Heligo—out of Heligoland!	O'Brien and Morse	1918
We're Going Over	Sterling, Grossman, and Lange	1917
What a Wonderful Dream It Would Be	Charles K. Harris	1918
When I Send You a Picture of Berlin	Fay, Ryan, and Dreyer	1918
When the Yanks Yank the Kaiser Off the Throne	Words by Robinette on American airs	1918
When Yankee Doodle Learns to Parlez Vous Francais	Hart and Nelson	1917
When You Come Back	George M. Cohan	1918
Where Do We Go From Here	Johnson and Wenrich	1917
Would You Rather Be a Colonel With an Eagle on His Shoulder Or a Private With a Chicken on His Knee?	Mitchell and Gottler	1918
A Yankee Doodle Boy Is Good Enough for Me	Livernash	1916
Your Lips Are No Man's Land But Mine	Guy Empey	1918

CHAPTER 6

The Cover Artists

It is a foregone conclusion that were it not for their attractive covers, song sheets would have less interest to the collector. Ironic though it seems, to the ordinary collector, the music itself appears to be secondary.

The name of Norman Rockwell needs no introduction, and his covers are the most coveted. To begin with, there were few Norman Rockwell song sheets issued. "Over There," "Little Grey Mother of Mine," "Down Where the Lillies Grow," and the later "Lady Bird Cha Cha Cha" are the only ones familiar to me. (They are reproduced by permission of Life Publishing Company.) This scarcity, coupled with Rockwell's popularity as *Saturday Evening Post* artist, accounts for the high prices being paid for his song sheets. There are few remaining, relatively speaking, and they are rapidly being absorbed into collections.

Noted illustrators, Archie Gunn, Hamilton King, and James Montgomery Flagg, have also appeared as song sheet cover artists, but they are rarities. Archie Gunn illustrated the cover of "The American Girl March" by Victor Herbert in the supplement to the *Examiner*. Hamilton King's cover appears on the song sheet of "Peggy O'Neil"; James Montgomery Flagg did the cover of "Father of the Land We Love" by George M. Cohan. A recent addition to my collection is the song sheet "Adoring You" (from the Ziegfeld Follies of 1924). The cover art work is by Albert Vargas who with "Petty" was known for "pin-up" girl illustrations circa 1940.

Nearly half of all song sheet covers were unsigned. Whether or not research will prove fruitful in attributing these covers to any particular artist belongs to the future. Rich in artistry, the unsigned category cannot be discounted. The title of Ugliest Cover should, in my opinion, go to the song "Smiles." A song of this caliber was deserving of a much better fate. The work was left unsigned, a wise decision.

As with the unsigned artist category, the miscellaneous artist category should not be ignored. Outstanding covers in both instances are plentiful. I have discovered over one hundred fifty different artists' signatures on large and standard song sheets.

One must not mistake the signature on a singing, movie, stage, or Vaudeville star's photograph for an artist's signature. It is merely the name of the photographer's studio. "Alpeda" is a good example; he photographed many star personalities for the song sheets. Look elsewhere on the cover for the artist's signature.

Could it have been the artistic nature of the man that prompted him to blend his signature into his work? I doubt it. I'm positive the sole purpose was to confuse me. J. V. R. among others is very guilty. Look in the bark of a tree, in flowers, in the woodwork, or any unlikely spot. One does develop an eye for it.

STARMER

Versatility was a requisite of the old song sheet cover artists. The most prolific of these was Starmer. His signature appears on twice the number of song sheets as any other cover artist. His artistry covered a period of, unbelievably, nearly half a century. The earliest Starmer cover I have encountered is 1897; the latest is 1944. A fountain of originality was he; be it comical covers, landscapes or portraits, he was equal to the task. Even the later Art Deco proved no great challenge to this giant. From the delightful "Oh, You Beautiful Doll" of the big hat to "Cruel Papa," his adaptability to a particular medium was proved again and again. Starmer ranks with Irving Berlin as one who contributed the most in his profession over the longest period of time. Starmer covers are a fertile field.

*Starmer Cover
Samples*

At the End of the Road	Doctor Brown
Blame It on the Blues	Doo Dah Blues
Cruel Papa	Fifty Fifty
Dixie Dimples	French Pastry Rag

ALBERT BARBELLE

Next to Starmer in productivity, Albert Barbelle must take the honors. The most prolific years of his artistry were the twenties.

The "Red Wing" standard sized song sheet cover was a Barbelle creation. (There was an earlier 1909 issue.) It was the haunting beauty of this cover that compelled me to research song sheet covers, which later encompassed the entire Tin Pan Alley spectrum.

Barbelle
Cover Samples

ANDRE DETAKACS

After viewing a hundred or more of Andre deTakacs' song sheet covers, uppermost in my mind was his inability to decide how best to sign his name. From a slanted "deTakacs" during his early years to his face signature of the latest song sheet in my collection, he seemed to experiment continually with his name.

I was left with the impression that he wanted to make a man's face of his signature from the very beginning and finally succeeded on "I'm Always Chasing Rainbows" of 1928.

Although quantitatively he did not compare with Starmer and Barbelle, his covers are unique. From the patriotic impact of his World War I covers to his cubistic "Pork and Beans," one is impressed with the quality of his work. Quality, not quantity, was deTakacs' trademark. He is my favorite.

*DeTakacs
Song Samples*

Alice Where Art Thou Going?
America Here's My Boy
Carbarlick Acid Rag
Golden Butterflies
The Gravel Rag
Hello Bill
Humpty Dumpty

The Midnight Whirl (Rag)
Pork and Beans
Put on Your Old Grey Bonnet
That's a Plenty
When Old Bill Bailey Plays the
   Ukelele

PFEIFFER

Like deTakacs, Pfeiffer will be remembered for his spectacular covers. The majority in my collection were on Waterson, Berlin, and Snyder Publishing Company issues. Two portraits, decorated in black, red, and white, prove attractive for framing. "Beautiful Eyes" and "I'm Going to Do What I Please" are both by Pfeiffer. His "Whoop 'Er Up" song sheet cover by Will Woods Publishing Company is prized highly. In addition, three outstanding covers are "Snookey Ookum's," "You're So Different From the Rest," and "Battle in the Sky." Pfeiffer song sheet covers are much to be desired.

Pfeiffer Samples

Battle in the Sky
Beautiful Eyes
Florentine Waltz
In the Heart of the City That
　Has No Heart
My Dream Train

Ragtime Violin
Snookey Ookums
That International Rag
Whoop 'Er Up
You're So Different From the
　Rest

JOHN FREW

It's silly, of course, but the phrase "Frew did a few, too" comes to mind whenever his name pops up. In fact, John Frew did quite a few. A choice collector's item with a Frew signature is "The Bird on Nellie's Hat." Other than this, his covers, which are early Art Deco in substance, lack the appeal of the previously mentioned artists. More interesting ones may be discovered.

**FREDERICK S.
MANNING**

Surely among the loveliest song sheet covers are the mystical Manning portraits. An ethereal quality in the majority of cases puts Frederick S. Manning in a class apart. His beautifully clad ladies, and his preference for soft hues in roses, greens, and blues are a treat to behold.

Unlike other cover artists, Manning specialized. It is not usual to find a song sheet by Manning without a beautiful lady, although they do exist. His landscapes, when found, display the same misty quality of his portraits. "They Gotta Quit Kicking My Dog Around" requires a second look, but his signature is there. This cover is comical in nature and out of keeping with his usual work.

Manning Song Samples

Ain't You Ashamed
At Twilight Time
Beautiful Annabelle Lee
California
Dreamer of Dreams
Hiawatha's Melody of Love
The Lovelight in Your Eyes

My Best Girl
My Buddy
Springtime
Wander With Me to Loveland
Why Couldn't It Be Poor Little
Me

OTHER NOTEWORTHY ARTISTS

R. S.

A stylized rose underscored with R. S. is a mystery to me. The use of the rose coupled with the first initial "R" leads me to believe the first name was "Rose," but there is no other clue.

This artist, like Starmer, decorated song sheets over a long period of time. The covers show adeptness and originality on large, small, and standard song sheets. The comical covers are outstanding.

R. S. Song Samples

At the High Brown Baby's Ball
Bow Wow Blues
I Don't Want to Get Well
I Used to Call Her Baby
It's Not Your Personality

Keep Your Eye on the Girlie
You Love
Marie, Marie, Marie
Pip Pip Toot Toot Goodbye-ee
Valse Mauve

Carter, Myers, Pryor

There was great satisfaction in solving the mystery of a signature comparable to a TV aerial. After viewing forty such signatures, I discovered two had the name "Carter" attached.

The Cover Artists

My confidence was shattered when, after a year and a half had lapsed, I found in a group of song sheets, two TV aerial signatures, one with the name "Myers" adjoining, the other with "Pryor!" My conclusion is that the TV aerial signature belongs to the studio, and Carter, Myers, and Pryor were the studio artists.

Carter, Myers,
Pryor Song Sheet
Cover Samples

Blue Bell
Good-Night Little Girl, Good-
    Night
Missouri Waltz

The Moon Has His Eyes on You
Under the Anheuser Bush
When You Wore a Pinafore

Gene Buck

Besides being a song sheet cover artist, Gene Buck was a successful lyricist and played an active role as president of ASCAP. His covers tend to be a bit austere, somewhat reminiscent of John Frew but without Frew's Art Deco inclination. His signature never varied; it is easily recognizable in plain block letters.

Gene Buck
Song Covers

As Long as the Shamrocks Grow
    Green
Everybody's Doin' It Now
General Grant's March
I Want to Be in Dixie

Last Night Was the End of the
    World
When a Fellow Who Is Lone-
    some Meets a Girl Who's
    Feeling Blue

ART DECO AND CARTOON COVER ARTISTS OF THE TWENTIES AND THIRTIES

Although the previously mentioned Starmer, Barbelle, and R. S. contributed immensely on both large and standard size song sheets, a new breed of artists emerged in the twenties. Besides having an inherent feeling for Art Deco, a technique similar to the Sunday comics of the day is distinctly theirs.

J. V. R.

The most confusing of all who contributed greatly on standard sized song sheets is the signature of J. V. R.—alone or coupled with C. E. M. or R. E. or both. The fact that he created so many striking covers makes it all the more disconcerting. The only clue is that C. E. M. could possibly be C. E. Millard's initials.

J. V. R. Cover Samples

I'm All Broken Up Over You
I'm Gonna Dance Wit de Guy
   Dat Brung Me
Me No Speaka Good English
Mr. Radio Man

No Wonder
A Sailor's Sweetheart
Turkey in the Straw
What Does the Pussy Cat Mean
   When He Says Meouw

Signatures of the following artists vary little and are easily found. They are seldom initialed and simply written.

*Wohlman Cover Samples
(Excels at Art Deco)*

Hawaiian Nightingale
La Veeda
Red Nose Pete

Swanee Butterfly
Tenderly
True Blue Sam

Perret Cover Samples

Driftwood
Mindin' My Business
Nobody Else Can Love Me Like
   My Old Tomato Can

Red Hot Mama
Salt Your Sugar
You Better Keep Babying Baby

Griffith Cover Samples

China Girl
Dream House
Harem Eyes

The Hoodoo Man
I Wish I Knew
The Sneak

Leff Cover Samples

Got No Time
I Wanta Be Loved Like a Baby
Oh How I Miss You Tonight
The Sweetest Rose of All

Who'll Take The Place of the
   Songbird Now Gone
Yes, Sir, That's My Baby

*Pud Lane Cover
Samples*

I Faw Down and Go Boom
Me and the Man in the Moon
Mean to Me

She's Wonderful
Sweet Seventeen
Through

Politzer Cover Samples Daddy's Wonderful Pal   Steal a Little Kiss
                        Go 'Long Mule   That's What the Moon Said to
                        Montmatre Rose   Me
                        Side by Side

ATTRACTIVE COVERS BY MISCELLANEOUS ARTISTS

Large Song Sheet

All Aboard for Chinatown	Universal Art Studios
Blue Goose Rag	Dulin Studios
Caberavings	Natwick
Can't You Love Me	Irene Ewing
Childhood Joys	Edna Longest
Dance of the Bumblebees	Dittmar
Fawn Eyes	Henrich
The Georgia Grind	R. L.
Gold Dust Twins Rag	Crews Studios
Hunkatin	Herman Hieschaool
Hysterics Rag	Valentino
I'm Crying Just For You	Hirt
Just a Moment	Grigware
Kangaroo Hop	Einson
The Kangaroo Hop	F. E. Looney
La Quapa	S. Cahan
Lake of the Woods Waltz	CLO (Western Engraving Colortype Co.)
Morning Cy!	Grover
The Night Owls	Ed Maquie
The Pace That Kills	H. C. K.
Pink Poodle One Step	Dulin Studios
That Fascinating Waltz	Etherington

Standard Song Sheet

Bowl of Pansies	Jemoushek
Dancin' Dan	Pel Studios
Girl of Mine	Armstrong
Good Old Days	B. N.
I Don't Believe You	Bruyere
I Wanta Yes-Yes Baby!	Art Strader
Lady of the Nile	A. D. Brown—Art
Lazy River	F. Hyer
Lonesome Mama Blues	Ilah Kibbey
Make Me	H. H. Warner
Mr. Goshawful Loose in His Galloping Goose	Hubert Wood
Oh! What a Pal Was Mary	The Knapp Company

Standard Song Sheets
(cont'd)

Overalls
So Long Oo-Long
Sweetheart Land

H.
The Knapp Company
P. W. Read

ATTRACTIVE UNSIGNED SONG SHEETS

Large Song Sheet

All America March
By Heck
Candied Cherries Rag
Casey Jones
Crabapple Rag
Dicty Doo
Flight of the Airship
Frou Frou
Gee Whiz
Glory of Jamestown
Grace and Beauty Rag
Keep Movin' Cake Walk
Keep Your Foot on the Soft Pedal
Kiss Me Goodnight
La Polechinette
Mammy Jinny's Hall of Fame

Meadow Lark Rag
The Moonlight Waltz
San Francisco the Paris of the
   U. S. A.
The Six Cylinder Kid
Sweetie Dear Fox Trot
Tears of Love
They Go Wild Simply Wild Over
   Me
They Start the Victrola
Tom Tom
When You and I Were Young,
   Maggie (Early issue)
World Peace
Yankiana

Standard Song Sheet

The Alcoholic Blues
Chiquita
Cross Patch
Dan, That Lovin' Sailor Man
I'm Just a Lonely Little Kid
I'm Living a Life of Shadow
In My Bouquet of Memories
In Sweet September
Last Night I Dreamed You
   Kissed Me

Little Pal of Long Ago
Melody of Love
Old Man Sunshine
Organ Grinder's Swing
Please
Sleepy Hollow
So Disappointed in You
That Wonderful Mother of Mine
When Lights Are Low

CHAPTER 7

Special
Covers

E. T. PAULL LITHOS

ow!" This slang expression of the younger generation properly describes my shock on first viewing an E. T. Paull song sheet.

E. T. Paull, composer of marches, arranger and publisher (he later formed the Paull-Pioneer Publishing Company) overshadowed the competition with his brilliant five-color lithographed song sheet covers. Extremely popular and rightfully so, they were executed by the A. Hoen Lithograph Company. One wonders who the artist was. A palette of red, turquoise, brown, yellow, and green, coupled mainly with violent action was the final result.

I am not aware at present of any other song sheet cover bearing the stamp of the A. Hoen Company. Realistically speaking, the credit should go to this company, but to avoid confusion, I will follow the established practice and refer to them as "Paull Lithos."

On the reverse of a standard 1922 reissue are advertised thirty-seven magnificently lithographed songs by E. T. Paull Publishing Company, which are listed here. All but six are marches. They were almost solely Paull compositions, although on twelve he collaborated with others. In these cases, Paull was probably the arranger. In "Midnight Fire Alarm," Harry J. Lincoln wrote the music and Paull the arrangement.

Although more prevalent than Norman Rockwell covers, they are in the scarce category. When found, they are normally ragged and dirty, which attests to their popularity. A complete collection of Paull Lithos would be more than worthy of the search, and most likely destined to increase considerably in value.

Paull Lithos

America Forever March
Arizona March
Ben Hur Chariot Race
The Burning of Rome
Charge of the Light Brigade
Circus Parade March and Two
   Step
Custer's Last Charge

Dance of the Fire Flies
Dawn of the Century March
The Flash-Light March
Four Horsemen of the
   Apocalypse
The Home Coming March
The Hurricane March
Ice Palace March and Two Step

Paull Lithos (cont'd)

The Jolly Blacksmith
Legion of Victory
Lincoln Centennial Grand
  March
The Masquerade March and
  Two-Step
Midnight Fire Alarm
The Midnight Flyer
Napoleon's Last Charge
New York and Coney Island
  Cycle March
Paul Revere's Ride
Race Course March

Romany Rye
Sheridan's Ride
Signal From Mars
Silver Sleigh Bells
Spirit of the U. S. A.
The Storm King
Stranger's Story Waltz
Triumphant Banner March
Uncle Jasper's Jubilee
Warming Up in Dixie
We'll Stand By the Flag March
Witch's Whirl Waltzes
Ziz, March and Two-Step

ART DECO (1910 TO 1935)

Garlands of flowers, baskets of fruit, poplar trees, fountains and nudes, geometric designs, masked harlequins, jesters and clowns, long-legged beauties with billowy skirts, stylized deers, flowers and greyhounds, streamlined human figures in exaggerated positions often in a state of movement as if caught by a candid camera, and finally cubism—flavor this mixture with Egyptian, American Indian, Mexican, and African condiments. These are the ingredients of Art Deco.

Just as Art Nouveau was a revolution against traditional art, Art Deco (Art Moderne) revolted against its predecessor—Art Nouveau and its preoccupation with and overemphasis on the curve.

As shown on song sheet covers, between 1910 and 1920, the old standby cover artist such as Starmer, Pfeiffer, R. S., DeTakacs, and Frew played an active role in the development of Art Deco. By the twenties, new names were popping up on Art Deco song sheet covers. C. E. Millard, Wohlman, G. Kraus, Perret, Politzer, and Griffith were important contributors to this field. C. E. Millard and Wohlman seemed to have caught best the feeling of Art Deco.

C. Luckyth Robert's "Pork and Beans" is considered in the scarce category. The cover artist was an old standby, Andre deTakacs. It is the sole example of cubism in my collection, or as a matter of record, viewed by me anywhere.

112

Special Covers   The current revival of interest in Art Deco shows no sign
of abatement. This style of art is well represented on the song
sheet covers, both large and standard size.

Art Deco Song Covers

Large Size

Ballin' the Jack	deTakacs
Cabaret Rag	Pfeiffer
Can't You Love Me	Irene Ewing
Everybody Loves Rag	Pfeiffer
Frou-Frou	Unsigned
Gee Whiz	Unsigned
The Kangaroo Hop	F. E. Looney
Keep Your Eye on the Girlie You Love	R. S.
Let's Go	Starmer
Pork and Beans	deTakacs
Sweetie Dear	Unsigned
Tiddle-de-Winks	Starmer
Whose Pretty Baby Are You Now	Starmer

Standard Size

Annabelle	Wohlman
Dream House	P. M. Griffith
I Like to Do It	C. E. Millard
In My Bouquet of Memories	Unsigned
Just a Gigolo	Unsigned
Kiss a Miss	Van Doorn Morgan
Let Me Call You Sweetheart	Mary Kidder
Love Is Just a Flower	Starmer
Mindin' My Bus'ness	Perret
Mystery	L. S. Reiss
Oh Vera!	G. Kraus
Second Hand Rose	Wohlman
Sweet Patootie Sal	Starmer
Tenderly	Wohlman
There Never Was a Girl Like Mary	Pell Studio
You Said Something When You Said Dixie	Wohlman

CARTOONISTS   As Tin Pan Alley is to music, so the Sunday Funnies are to
art. Both are innovations of the U. S. A.

Covers by eminent cartoonists are so scarce that I have
grouped them under one heading. Opper, Billy DeBeck, Clare

*Introducing the
Song Sheet*

Victor Dwiggins, Swinnerton, Gaar Williams, Paul Fung, George McManus, and Harold Grey are the most familiar. The song sheets bearing their respective signatures are scarce, indeed. Those listed here are from the author's collection.

Song Title	*Cartoonist*	*Comic Strip*
Barney Google	DeBeck	Barney Google
Bringing Up Father	George McManus	Bringing Up Father
Come on Sparkplug!	DeBeck	Barney Google
Dreaming of You	Paul Fung (None of his are cartoon types)	Dumb Dora
Happy Hooligan	Opper	Happy Hooligan, Gloomy Gus, Alphonse and Gaston
Little Orphan Annie	Harold Gray	Little Orphan Annie
Long Boy	Gaar Williams	Unknown
Ophelia Rag	Clare Victor Dwiggins	Ophelia
Seattle Town	Paul Fung	Dumb Dora
So I Took the $5,000	DeBeck	Barney Google
There's a Dark Man Coming With a Bundle	Swinnerton	Tumble Tom, Bunny Schultze, and Foxy Grandpa

LINENS

Surviving extraordinarily well under the constant usage common to song sheets are what have been referred to as the "linens," issued in both large and standard size.

A high quality white, minutely pebbled surface with a matte finish distinguishes the linens from other song sheets. A variety of flowers graced the linens, with roses the overwhelming favorite. An occasional landscape may be found, but whatever the subject, it was always tastefully executed.

Carrie Jacobs-Bond & Sons and Sam Fox Publishing Co. appear to share equally in the use of linens to print sheet music.

Linen Cover Samples

Large Size			
	Betty's Music Box	Carrie Jacobs-Bond	1917
	Basket of Roses	Fred G. Albers	1913
	A Cottage in God's Garden	Carrie Jacobs-Bond	1917

114

Large Size (cont'd)	The Shepherdess	Archibald Sullivan and Carrie Jacobs-Bond	1910
	Today	John Bennett and Carrie Jacobs-Bond	1915
Standard Size	The Golden Key	Carrie Jacobs-Bond	1924
	I Love You Truly	Carrie Jacobs-Bond	1906
	Lazy River	Carrie Jacobs-Bond	1923
	A Mother's Croon	Edson and Walt	1921
	Nola	Burns and Arndt	1915
	Out of the Dusk To You	Lamb and Lee	1922

SUNDAY SUPPLEMENTS

In the days when the microphone was unheard of, promoters attempted to popularize a song by issuing supplemental song sheets with the Sunday paper. In stark contrast to the linens, "Sunday supplements" were issued on the cheapest of paper. The years have played havoc with these song issues, leaving them yellowed and brittle, the outer edges eaten away. Mere handling is hazardous to the Sunday supplements, which seem literally to fall apart.

Why collect these often motheaten relics? First, because they are relics. Secondly, the covers, ordinarily comical in nature, are, one must assume, drawn by cartoonists on the staff of the paper with which they were issued. The song "There's a Dark Man Coming With a Bundle" has a cover by Swinnerton, an eminent cartoonist of that era. He was the creator of Tumble Tom, Bunny Schultze, and Foxy Grandpa. Another unsigned supplement appears to be by Opper since the song is "Happy Hooligan March and TwoStep." Happy Hooligan was an Opper creation. Certainly others will be discovered. One other Sunday supplement artist whose name appears frequently is J. B. Eddy, the illustrator of note.

The Sunday supplement songs were often composed expressly for the newspapers. They are a good source for musical stars and musical shows, provided they *survive* the trip home.

My earliest issue is Victor Herbert's "American Girl March," dated 1895. It was published in a smaller than normal size, of better quality paper, and under a cover far more colorful than usual. Archie Gunn the noted illustrator is the artist. In 1896 an even smaller size supplement was issued. Graham's "When the Little Ones Are Coming Home From School" is about equal in quality and color to Gunn's work. It was not signed by an artist.

The Sunday supplements covered a period approximating twelve years, from 1895 to 1908, although a late bloomer issued by the *Honolulu Star Bulletin* is dated 1923. Reputedly this practice was unsuccessful, and yet would the supplements have continued for that long a period without benefit? Habit at times supersedes common sense.

Sunday Supplement
Cover Samples

Song	*Cover Artist*
American Girl March	Archie Gunn
Happy Hooligan	Opper (Assumed)
Honey ($1,000 prize song)	Unsigned
I Caught You Making Eyes at Me	H. B. Eddy
Maudie (Josephine Cohan photo)	Clifton
My Dandy Soldier Coon (May Irwin)	Unsigned
Prancing Pickaninnies (Cake walk)	Unsigned
There's a Dark Man Coming With a Bundle	Swinnerton
When the Little Ones Are Coming Home From School	Unsigned

ADVERTISING
SONG SHEETS

If your forte is advertising song sheets, a scarce and prized plum is "Wait For The Wagon." This extraordinary song sheet was published by the Studebaker Brothers, and complimentary copies were distributed for the New Year of 1884. A finely colored lithograph by Gugler Company shows the four Studebaker Brothers, their birthplace in Adams County, Pennsylvania, and a horse drawn wagon loaded with New Year's revelers. On the reverse is printed "A Carol of the Studebaker Wagon," lauding its virtues and telling of its birth. It is a four-versed parody of "Wait For the Wagon." (An excellent copy is co-owned by me, but that is another story.)

Sixty-five years later in 1941, a free song sheet called "Honeymoon For Three" was your invitation to view the new Chevrolet. The Honeymoon's third party was the automobile.

In all probability, the Garland Stove Company was the first to take advantage of the song sheet as an advertising medium on an extensive scale. An example is "Little Annie Rooney." It was written in 1889; the cover is a black and white lithograph.

Following quickly on the heels of Garland Stove Company, was the Bromo Seltzer Company, which boasted 171 song selections, mostly standards and hymns. These were distributed to local pharmacies throughout the country. By submitting a two-cent stamp and a Bromo Seltzer wrapper, you could select two songs, plus of course, you could "Try this over on your piano" without ever suffering a headache!

"Miss Samantha Johnson's Wedding Day" holds the dubious honor of being the song sheet most nearly covered by advertisers. It is not an advertising song sheet in the strictest sense but was obviously stamped over by a multitude of advertisers. Every available border or vacant space was used by twenty separate advertisers—even to the point of obliterating portions of the music.

True advertising song sheets, published by the various companies or expressly for the companies, are not commonly found and are much sought after.

Giving song sheets as a promotional scheme must have attained a good degree of success since the practice has been continued to some extent through the entire Tin Pan Alley era and later.

Advertising Song Sheet Samples

Song	Advertiser	Year
Bromo Seltzer songs	Bromo Seltzer	circa 1890
Cable March and Two Step	Cable Piano Company	1903
Garland Stove Company songs	Garland Stove Company	circa 1890
The Greater Seattle March and Twostep	Standard Furniture Company Seattle	1910
Honeymoon for Three	Chevrolet Automobile	1949
The Merry Singer	Singer Manufacturing Company	1891
Milena Two Step	Huntington Piano Company	1910
Song of the Great Big Baked.Potato	Northern Pacific Railroad	Before 1918
Wait For The Wagon (Originally written during the Civil War)	Studebaker Wagons	1884
Way Down Upon the Suwanee River	Southern Railway System	1921
Wiley B. Allen's Progressive March	The Wiley B. Allen Music Store	1890

**COWBOY AND
ACTION WESTERNS**

A brief mention here should be made regarding song covers depicting the "wild West."

Although scarcity is an important aspect in the collecting field, one must not conclude that availability alone dictates price, since many factors enter into the picture. The development of the West has always held an enormous fascination for Americans. The "action Western" song sheet covers, reminiscent of Russell and Remington, are the most desirable. These covers are attractive and colorful. There are but three in my collection, which numbers in the thousands. I predict that action Westerns are destined to increase in value and interest.

The titles listed here are all large sized song sheets.

Song Title	Cover Artist
Broncho Buster	Unknown
Cheyenne	Illegible
Cowboy	Unknown
In the Land of the Buffalo	Unknown
Santa Fe Song	Starmer
Whoop 'er Up	Pfeiffer

CHAPTER 8

The Entertainment Field

rior to the motion picture films, American musical entertainment came in many forms. The earliest were the minstrel shows that predated the Alley by at least thirty-five years, which places their origin in approximately the 1840s. By the 1880s, the varieties took over; they were in turn succeeded by the operettas, Vaudeville, and the extravaganzas such as follies, revues, scandals, and others. These finally evolved into our present Broadway musicals.

MUSICAL SHOWS

These musical entertainment forms were all at one time or another contemporaneous with Tin Pan Alley. Because the singing star and the songs were interdependent, the various genre of music-related shows became interwoven with the Alley. Their life blood intermingling, each contributed to the common cause of prepetuating the show and its songs. The musicals were all advertised on the covers of their associated songs.

Perhaps the most famous of the musicals, the Ziegfeld Follies, was in existence from 1907 until 1943. Irving Berlin's Music Box Revues were performed from 1921 to 1924. Some of the other famous variety shows included George White's Scandals, the Greenwich Village Follies, Jack Norworth's Odds and Ends, the Hippodrome Shows, Earl Carroll Vanities, Schubert's Passing Shows, the Wintergarden Shows, and the Broadway Brevities.

In addition there were the following big-name musical entertainment producers: Oliver Morosco, Henry Savage, Mort Singer, Daniel Arthur, Lew Fields, Whitney, Charles Dillingham (the Hippodrome), Klaw and Erlander, George W. Lederer, Richard Carle, Joe Hertig, and August Pitou.

Samples of musical shows advertised on pre–1920 song sheets

George M. Cohan

Fifty Miles From Boston	Hello Broadway
Forty-Five Minutes to Broadway	Little Johnny Jones
George Washington Jr.	Running for Office
The Governor's Son	The Talk of New York

Victor Herbert Operettas

The Belle of Avenue A	The Gold Bug
The Fortune Teller	Naughty Marietta

Victor Herbert Operettas (cont'd)	Prince Ananias	The Wizard of the Nile
	The Red Mill	
Others	The Beauty Shop	Cohan and Harris
	The Big Show Hippodrome	Dillingham
	The Boys and Betty	Arthur
	In Central Park	Klaw and Erlander
	The Chocolate Soldier	B. C. Whitney
	The Fascinating Widow	Woods
	Follow Me	Anna Held
	George Washington Bullion Abroad	The Smart Set Company
	Higgledy Piggeldy	Weber and Ziegfeld
	In London	Klaw and Erlander
	A Knight for a Day	B. C. Whitney
	Little Miss Fixit	Werba and Lueshers
	Maid in America	Winter Garden
	Mary's Lamb	Richard Carle
	O'Neill of Derry	Chauncy Olcott
	Over the River	Chas. Dickson
	Peg o' My Heart	Morosco
	The Rounders	George Lederer
	Sergeant Kitty	George R. White
	Sin'Bad	Wintergarden Show
	So Long, Letty	Morosco
	The Spring Chicken	Richard Carle
	Suzie	Lew Field
	The Tik-Tok Man of Oz	Morosco
	The Time, the Place and the Girl	Mort Singer
	A Yankee Tourist	Savage

Post–1920s Samples

The Cat and the Fiddle	Porgy and Bess
Criss Cross	Rainbow
The Desert Song	Roberta
Hit the Deck	Rose Marie
Lucky	Two Little Girls in Blue
No, No, Nanette	Wild Flower

STARS—
COON SHOUTERS
AND OTHERS

Sung with great success by/ prominently featured by/ introduced and sung by the phenomenal/ triumphantly featured by/ and sung with tremendous success by/ were descriptive phrases coupled with an eminent star's photograph found on many old song sheets during the late 1800s and early 1900s.

When the radio and phonograph were but in the experimental stage, minstrel shows, stage shows, and Vaudeville were the only avenues of song-plugging open to the music publishing business. The association of any song with a particular star performer virtually assured its success. Consequently, every publisher or song plugger used all means at his disposal in convincing a star to include a song in his or her repertoire. This included giving anything from costly jewelry to a percentage of the song's take and was "payola" in its rudimentary stage. It was also the happy wedding of the song and the singer—each completely dependent on the other for survival.

Does the name Lillian Russell sound familiar? Of course, but mainly because her life story was the subject of movies, books, and stage shows. How about Nora Bayes? She's probably less well known. But you will possibly remember Anne Sheridan who played Nora Bayes in *Shine on Harvest Moon.* Lillian Russell and Nora Bayes, plus a host of other stars, were the darlings of their day—idolized, adored, and catered to.

Coon songs were the end result of the minstrel shows and enjoyed great popularity at this time. Early songbirds who specialized in coon songs were referred to as "coon shouters." They had little in common with modern singers. Their popularity as entertainers depended on their ability to overwhelm an audience by the sheer power of their voices. Husky throated contraltos, whether they sang tear-jerkers or coon songs, left an auditorium of people emotionally drained.

The reason is obscure, but at the same time lady contraltos were musically fashionable, male tenors were also enjoying popularity. A different breed were the minstrel shows that were a carryover from the Civil War. The entire cast consisted of male members whose success lay in their ability to best personify the popular caricature of the Negro in song and dance.

They often worked in pairs, like Primrose and West. The culmination of this "coon" type of impersonation was not reached until the early 1900s when America discovered Al Jolson. The rest is legendary, for every generation since has rediscovered him.

The old song sheets are a treasure trove of these singers. In most cases a song was made by a star's rendition, and conversely a singer became successful by the introduction of a particular song.

Some stars of note prior to the age of movies, phonograph, and radio enjoyed success over a long enough time to become a part of both eras. Sophie Tucker is a case in point.

Several women stars of this period were nicknamed for their more conspicuous qualities. The "Queen Regent of Song" was *Imogene Comer,* also known as the "Big Voice." *May Irwin* was considered the "Stage Mother of Ragtime." She popularized the famous "Bully Song." *Maggie Cline,* with a voice described as Stentorian, was known for her "Throw 'Em Down McClosky" song. *Lottie Gilson* was called the "Little Magnet" because she was such a draw at the box office. Songwriter Jim Thornton's wife was *Lizzie Cox,* the "Little Mascot." The "Aristocrat of Lady Vaudevillians" was *Nora Bayes,* who was also "Queen of the Coon Shouters" and "The Wurzburger Girl." She co-authored "Shine on Harvest Moon" with her husband Jack Norworth. *Lillian Russell* was, of course, a legend. *May Howard* was the first of the burlesque queens and Paul Dresser's wife for a short time. The title "Queen of Venuses" went to *Lillian Lorraine. Anna Held* was so famous in her heyday that Flo Ziegfeld was known as Anna Held's husband. *Louise Dresser* took Paul Dresser's name in appreciation for his assistance in promoting her career. *Eva Tanguay* was nicknamed the "I Don't Care" girl, "Miss Tobasco," and "The Human Gyroscope." *Sophie Tucker* is famous as the "Last of the Red Hot Mammas." *Winona Winter's* father composed "White Wings." *Karyl Norman* was designated the "Creole Fashion Plate." *Maude Nugent* wrote "Sweet Rosy O'Grady." *Fanny Bryce* is known to modern movie-goers as "Funny Girl." *Blanche Ring* and *Helen Mora* are other women singers of the pre-movie era.

The male singing stars seem to have had fewer nicknames. A major exception was George M. Cohan, the "Singing Patriot." Francis X. Bushman was voted "Pin-up boy" by *National* magazine. Arthur Monday was known as a society entertainer. Other stars include: Raymond Teal, Warren and Blanchard, Ed Morton, Al Jolson, Raymond Hitchcock, John Steel, Billy Gaston, Eddie Leonard, Gus Williams, Weber and Field, Dick Jose, Billy West, George Primrose, Barney Fagan, Pan Rooney, Eddie Foy, Richard Carle, Harry Lauder, Lew Dockstader, Sam Bernard and Ted Lewis.

**Stars—
Coon Shouters
and Others**

Song Title	Featured Star
Alabama Jubilee	Elizabeth Murray
All She'd Say Was Umh-hum	Van and Schenck
Baby Sister Blues	Duncan Sisters
Belle of the Bathers	Richard Carle
A Bird in a Gilded Cage	Frank Standish
Bring Along Your Dancing Shoes	Al Jolson
'Bye and Bye	Wright and Dietrich
Daisies Will Tell You So	Anita Owen
Darktown Strutters' Ball	Sophie Tucker
Don't Bite the Hand That's Feeding You	Ed Morton
Elsie From Chelsea	Bonnie Thornton
For Old Times Sake	Warren and Blanchard
Gee, But It's Great to Meet a Friend From Your Home Town	Sadie Helf
Georgette	Ted Lewis
Girls, Girls, Girls	Marie Cahill
Honolulu Eyes	Avon Comedy Four
I Ain't Got Nobody	Sophie Tucker
I Love a Lassie	Harry Lauder
I Never Knew I Could Love Anybody	Jane Green
I Want to Know Where Tosti Went	Bert Williams
I'd Love to Live in Loveland	Maud Lambert
I'll Dig a Subway to Your Heart	Arthur Monday
I'll Get You	George Jessel, Ethel Movey
I'll Say She Does	Al Jolson
Isle d'Amour	Jose Collins
It's Nice to Get Up in the Morning	Harry Lauder

I've a Garden in Sweden	Nora Bayes
I've Been Floating Down That old Green River	Florence Moore
Kiss Me My Honey, Kiss Me	Amy Butler
Ma Lady Lu	Charles B. Ward
Mamie Reilly	Maude Nugent
Meet Me Tonight in Dreamland	Reine Davies
My Irish Senorita	Eddie Foy
My Melancholy Baby	June LeVeay
My Own Iona	Elizabeth Brice and Charles King
'N' Everything	Al Jolson
Nancy Clancy	Anna Held
Not Yet Suzette	Brooke Johns and Anne Pennington
Oh Johnny! Oh Johnny! Oh!	Nora Bayes
Oh Kitty	Virginia Earl
Peachie	Emily Miles
Peg o' My Heart	Laurette Taylor
Play That Barber Shop Chord	Bert Williams
Red Moon	Genevieve Tobin
Redhead	Irene Franklin
She's My Warm Baby	Flo Irwin
Somebody Loves Me (By Hattie Starr)	Josephine Sabel
Stories Mother Told Me	Julie Mackey
Swanee	Al Jolson
Sweet Italian Love	Irving Berlin
Sweet Suzanne	Henry Santrey
Take Plenty of Shoes	Marie Cahill
This Is the Life	Al Jolson
Under Any Old Flag at All	George M. Cohan
Waiting For a Certain Girl	Richard Carle
The Way to Kiss	Lulu Glazer
The Wedding Glide	Shirley Kellog
The Wee Hoose Mang the Heather	Harry Lauder
What Do You Want to Make Those Eyes at Me For	Emma Carus
When You Come Back	George M. Cohan
When You Dream of the Girl You Love	Bessie Wynne
When You're All Dressed Up and No Place to Go	Raymond Hitchcock
Where the Black-Eyed Suzans Grow	Al Jolson

Who Paid the Rent for   Sam Bernard
   Mrs. Rip Van Winkle
You're More Than the World to Me   Nonette

SONGS OF
THE SILENTS

It is sheer irony that a song in a sense contributed to the Alley's undoing (see Chapter 1). The song was "Little Lost Child," by Ed Marks and Joe Stern. In 1895 or thereabout, Ed Marks conceived the idea and, with the aid of an electrician, developed a plan to photograph actors and actresses in subsequent portrayals of poignant episodes from this tear-jerker. These then were placed on slides and projected through a lantern onto a screen while the song was being sung. Immediately successful, the lantern slide and the song became synonymous. Later came the silent movie and the theme song, eventually followed by synchronization of musical score and film, and finally there were the "Talkies."

In 1926 Warner Brothers purchased a device called the "Vitaphone." It synchronized a wax sound recording with a film projector. That same year Warners produced the movie *Don Juan* with a musical score. In 1927 Al Jolson sang songs in *The Jazz Singer*. The first *all talk* film, *Lights of New York,* was produced in 1928 by Warner Brothers' Vitaphone process. William Fox used a similar device called "Movietone."

Silent movie theme song covers advertised the movie with which they were associated. The stars of the film were normally shown on the cover, along with the particular film company and the producer. The songs were often dedicated to the stars.

The first theme song attaining national popularity and written especially for a movie film was *Mickey* from Mack Sennett's 1918 photoplay of the same name, starring Mabel Normand. This song was issued in three different sizes, showing Mabel Normand in three separate poses. The large sized song sheet was published in 1918, the small in 1918, and the standard issued in 1919. There was an additional standard sized publication with Mabel Normand in another pose, making four distinct covers in all. Could there be more?

There are two avenues of approach, for collecting under the

"songs of the silents" category. First, there are song sheets definitely designated as a theme song or introduced in a motion picture. Secondly, one can collect by the silent stars pictured on the song sheets but not designated as connected with a movie film. Somewhere on the cover was usually printed: Photograph reproduced by permission of the film company with which the star was affiliated.

There is one major problem in connection with the "silents" category. During the transition period silents, semi-silents (films with musical scores or part "talkies"), and "talkies" were being produced. Any song sheet with "Vitaphone" and "Movietone" came from a movie with at least partial sound. The fact that the producers advertised their movies as "all talkies" is tremendously helpful, for example, Gloria Swanson in *The Trespasser,* a United Artists' all talking production that was made in 1929. One can assume that by 1930 there were no more silents, although Charlie Chaplin produced two films at a later date.

Songs of the Silents

Song	Stars	Movie	Film Company
Beggers of Life	Wallace Beery	Beggers of Life	Paramount
Charmaine	Dolores Del Rio	What Price Glory	William Fox
Diane	Janet Gaynor and Charles Farrell	Seventh Heaven	National Film Attraction
The Flapper Wife	Sylvia Breamer	The Flapper Wife	A First National Picture
The Girl of the Golden West	Harold Lloyd	The Girl of the Golden West	Pathe
Girl Shy	Vera Gordon and Bobby Connelly	Girl Shy	Paramount
Humoresque		Humoresque	
I'm Just a Lonely Little Kid	Jackie Coogan	My Boy	Unknown
Jeaninne, I Dream of Lilac Time	Colleen Moore	Lilac Time	First National Attraction
Just an Old Love Song	Douglas Fairbanks	Robin Hood	Unknown
Laugh, Clown, Laugh	Lon Chaney	Laugh, Clown, Laugh	Metro, Goldwyn, Mayer
The Lonesome Road		Showboat	Carl Laemmle's Universal
Mickey	Mabel Normand	Mickey	Mack Sennett
Moonlight on the Danube	Leatrice Joy	The Blue Danube	DeMille Pictures Corporation
My Wild Irish Rose		My Wild Irish Rose	Vitagraph
Neopolitan Nights	Charles Farrell and Greta Nissen	Fazil	William Fox
One Wonderful Night	Francis X. Bushman	One Wonderful Night	Essenay
Poor Pauline	Pearl White	Perils of Pauline	Pathe
Rainbow Isle		The Idol Dancer	D. W. Griffiths
Ramona	Dolores Del Rio	Ramona	United Artists
Rose of Monterey	Mary Astor and Gilbert Roland	Rose of the Golden West	A First National Picture
Salley of My Dreams	Madge Bellamy	Mother Knows Best	William Fox
Same Old Town		Same Old Town	Famous Players
School Days	Wesley Barry	School Days	Warner Brothers' Photoplay
Smilin' Through	Norma Talmadge	Smilin' Through	A First National Attraction
Your Goodbye Kiss	Johnny Burke and Sally Eilers	Your Goodbye Kiss	Mack Sennett

Silent Stars on Song Sheets

Song	Star	Film Company
Daddy Long Legs	Ruth Chatterton	
Daddy Mine	Mae Marsh	Goldwyn
The Gates of Gladness	Jean Paige and Denton Vane	Vitagraph
I'm Going to Follow the Boys	Gladys Leslie	Vitagraph
In the Heart of the Berkshire Hills	Alice Joyce	Vitagraph
A Land of Broken Dreams	Florence Vidor	Thomas H. Ince Studios
Lullaby Time	Mabel Normand	Goldwyn
Pauline Waltz	Pearl White	Pathe
The Red Lantern	Nazimova	Metro Pictures Corporation
That Wonderful Mother of Mine	Mrs. Jane Jennings	Vitagraph
Your Lips Are No Man's Land But Mine	Arthur Guy Empy	Vitagraph

Some Early Film Companies On Song Sheets

American
Biograph
Champion
DeMille Picture Corporation
Edison
Essanay Film Manufacturing Company
Famous Players Film Company

First National
William Fox
IMP
Kalem
Laemmles' Imp Company
Lubin
Mack Sennett
Majestic

National Film Attraction
Nestor
Pathe
Reliance
Selig
Thanhauser
Vitagraph

Important Stars of the Silents

Female

Jean Arthur
Vilma Banky
Theda Bara
Ethel Barrymore
Clara Bow
Billy Burke
Marie Cahill
Dolores Costello
Helen Costello
Bebe Daniels
Marion Davies
Marie Dressler
Madge Evans

Geraldine Farrar
Pauline Frederick
Greta Garbo
Janet Gaynor
Dorothy Gish
Lillian Gish
Mae Irwin
Alice Joyce
Florence Lawrence
Mae Marsh
Mary Miles Minter
Nazimova
Pola Negri

Mabel Normand
Mary Pickford
Zazu Pitts
Marjorie Rambeau
Norma Shearer
Gloria Swanson
Constance Talmadge
Norma Talmadge
Laurette Taylor
Pearl White
Lois Wilson
Clara Kimball Young

Roscoe (Fatty) Arbuckle
George Arliss
G. M. Anderson (First cowboy star)
King Baggot
John Barrymore
Lionel Barrymore
Richard Barthelmess
Wallace Beery
John Bunny
Francis X. Bushman
Harry Carey
Charles Chaplin
Ronald Coleman

Jackie Coogan
Maurice Costello
William Desmond
Arthur Guy Empey
Douglas Fairbanks
Dustin Farnham
Charles Farrell
W. C. Fields
John Gilbert
D. W. Griffith
William S. Hart
Sessue Hayakawa
Edward Everett Horton
J. Warren Kerrigan

Rod LaRocque
Harold Lloyd
Victor MacLaglen
Tom Mix
Tom Moore
Antonio Moreno
Frank Morgan
Ramon Navarro
Wallace Reid
Buddy Rogers
Mack Sennett
Ben Turpin
Rudolph Valentino

STARS OF RADIO RECORDS, AND THE TALKIES

In the post–silent screen era, radios and phonographs were still the new toys of the American people. The piano was almost totally ignored and the player piano considered outmoded and *passé*. After all, it took two feet to operate that contrivance. In contrast, the turn of a knob or twist of a crank could produce a symphony of sounds—even from the far corners of the earth! The movies—well, what was Saturday night without tickets to the latest talkie?

"Successfully featured by" was still a hangover phrase used on song sheets during the twenties in conjunction with a star and song. "Introduced by" or "as featured in," however, were quickly replacing this hackneyed term.

In many cases one is left completely uncertain about whether the cover star was connected with radio, record, or the movies. In many instances a star was a star of all mediums. Al Jolson, Eddie Cantor, and Sophie Tucker are a few examples.

The performers or movies were rapidly taking over the song sheet covers. This happily provides a gallery of stars to collect. Where else but on song sheets does one find such a vast array of stellar personalities, often colorfully reproduced? In addition to the individual performer, famous band leaders or entire bands were featured (another area for the collector).

The most sought after star is in all likelihood Al Jolson.

Charlie Chaplin, Shirley Temple, and Eddie Cantor are next in line. Because they were instrumental in popularizing so many hit songs, Al Jolson, Rudy Vallee, Bing Crosby, Sophie Tucker, and Ruth Etting covers are in plentiful supply. Do you remember Harry Richman? His photo appears on a host of song sheets. Bing Crosby, Shirley Temple, and Kate Smith were of the Tin Pan Alley era at the beginning of their careers, but their greatest degree of popularity was attained later.

An individual song was often issued with several different star personalities on the covers. "Bye, Bye, Blackbird" is a case in point. The four covers were identical, with the exception of the stars' photograph. Gus Edwards, Frank Richardson, Olive O'Niel, and the Angelus Sisters were the cover stars in this instance.

Song	*Cover Star*	*Movie*
Abdulabulbul Amir	Frank Crumit	
Ain't We Got Fun	George Watts (Watts and Hawley), Arthur West	
Allah	Mme. Nazimova	
Alma Mammy	Nancy Carroll, Jack Oakie	
Aren't We All	Janet Gaynor	*Sunny Side Up*
At Your Command	Bing Crosby	
Big Boy	Sophie Tucker	
The Blue of the Night	Bing Crosby	
Blues in the Night	Norma Shearer	*Their Own Desire*
By the Fireside	Rudy Vallee	
Bye Bye, Blackbird	Gus Edwards, Olive O'Niel, Frank Richardson, the Angelus Sisters	
Castle of Romance	Courtney Sisters	
Celia	Mary Brian and Richard Arlen	*The Man I Love*
Cherie, I love You	Grace Moore	
Clementine (From New Orleans)	Blossom Seely	
Cuban Love Song	Evelyn Laye	*Cuban Love Song*
Dancing with Tears in My Eyes	Rudy Vallee	
Don't Be Like That	Helen Kane	
Don't Leave Me Mammy	Vincent O'Donnell (The Kid McCormack)	

130

Song	Cover Star	Movie
Egyptian Ella	Ted Weems and Orchestra	
Every Night I Cry Myself to Sleep	Blossom Seely	
Everything I Have Is Yours	Clark Gable and Joan Crawford	*Dancing Lady*
Falling	Joseph Lertora	
Farewell	Douglas Fairbanks, Jr.	*Party Girl*
For My Baby	Ruth Etting	
Glad Rag Doll	Dolores Del Rio	*Glad Rag Doll*
Gee, But I Hate to Go Home Alone	White Sisters	
Here I am	Harry Richman	
I Love Louisa	Helen Kane	*The Band Wagon*
If You Want the Rainbow You Must Have the Rain	Fanny Bryce	*My Man*
If You Were the Only Girl in the World	Rudy Vallee	
I'll Be Faithful	Ruth Etting	
I'm Alone Because I Love You	Belle Baker	
I'm Cuckoo Over You	Sally Fields	
I'm Forever Blowing Bubbles	June Caprice	
I'm Just a Vagabond Lover	Rudy Vallee	
I'm Not Complaining	Morton Downey	
I'm Sitting High on a Hilltop	Dick Powell	*Thanks a Million*
I'm Walking Around in a Dream	Ted Lewis	
In a Shanty in Old Shanty Town	Alice Joy	
In My Little Hope Chest	Nancy Carroll	*Honey*
It's Easy to Remember	Bing Crosby and Joan Bennett	*Mississippi*
I've Been Waiting All My Life	Marion Sunshine	
Just a Year Ago Tonight	Kate Smith	
Just One More Chance	Ross Sisters	
Just You, Just Me	Marion Davies	*Marianne*
Kentucky Dream	Mabel Normand	
Let's Put Out the Lights and Go to Sleep	Rudy Vallee	
Little Pal	Al Jolson	*Say It With Songs*
Little White Lies	Tommy and Willie (WKRC radio and record stars) Vincent Lopez, Rudy Vallee	
Look in the Mirror	Eileen Stanley	
Louisville Lou	Sophie Tucker	

Song	Cover Star	Movie
Love Is Like That	Ruth Etting	
Love Thy Neighbor	Bing Crosby	*We're Not Dressing*
Love Your Spell Is Everywhere	Gloria Swanson	*The Trespasser*
Mama Goes Where Papa Goes	Ruth Raye	
Mandalay	Charlie Chaplin, Giersdorf Sisters	
Many Happy Returns of the Day	Allen Daniels	
Memories of One Sweet Kiss	Al Jolson and Davy Lee	*Say It With Songs*
Moonstruck	Bing Crosby	*College Humor*
Muddy Waters	Nora Bayes	
My Blue Heaven	Paul Whiteman	
My Man From Caroline	Ethel Merman	
My Song of the Nile	Richard Barthelmess	*Drag*
Nancy	John Steel	
The Night of Love	Vilma Bankey (Writer)	
Nobody Lied	Karyl Norman	
Now I Lay Me Down to Sleep	Jean Granese	
The Old Spinning Wheel	Paul Whiteman, Jack Denny	
One Pair of Pants at a Time	Ted Healey	*Soup to Nuts*
O-oo Ernest	Eddie Cantor	
Orange Blossom Time	Carole Lombard and others	*Hollywood Revue* (1929)
Out of the Blue	Dolores Del Rio	*Bird of Paradise*
Pagan Love Song	Ramon Navarro	*The Broadway Melody*
Painting the Clouds With Sunshine	Variety of stars	*Gold Diggers of Broadway*
Paradise	Pola Negri	*A Woman's Command*
Please	Bing Crosby	*The Big Broadcast*
Ragamuffin Romeo	Paul Whiteman	*King of Jazz*
Rio Rita	Bebe Daniels	*Rio Rita*
Rock-a-Bye Baby Blues	Kelley Sisters	
Roll 'em Girls	Bobby Heath Revue	
Rosalie	Nelson Eddy	*Rosalie*
Sahara	Esther Walker	
Sailing Away on the *Henry Clay*	Four Marx Brothers	
Say a Little Prayer for Me	Ruth Etting	
Shadow Waltz	Dick Powell	*Gold Diggers of 1933*
She'll Be Comin' Round the Mountain	Ben Bernie	
Shuffle Off to Buffalo	Seven separate stars	
Silver Haired Daddy of Mine	Gene Autry	*Tumbling Tumbleweed*

Song	Cover Star	Movie
Sippin' Cider Thru' a Straw	Fatty Arbuckle	
Smoke Gets in Your Eyes	Irene Dunne, Fred Astaire, Ginger Rogers	
So Blue	The Embassy Boys	
So Tired	Gene Austin	
Somebody's Wrong Song	Sophie Tucker	
Song o' My Heart	John McCormack	
Springtime in the Rockies	Rudy Vallee	
Sweet Mama	Jackson and Taylor	
Sweety Pie	Freddy Martin	
There Oughta Be a Moonlight Saving Time	Harry Richman	
There's Something About You	Al Jolson	
There's Yes, Yes in Your Eyes	Giersdorf Sisters	
This Is Heaven	Vilma Bankey	*This Is Heaven*
Three Little Words	Amos and Andy	*Three Little Words*
Tie Me to Your Apron Strings Again	Belle Hawley (Hawley and Watts)	
To Know You Is to Love You	Winnie Lightner and Joe E. Brown	*Hold Everything*
Twelfth Street	Buddy Rogers	*Close Harmony*
Under a Texas Moon	Frank Fay	*Under a Texas Moon*
Venetian Moon	Bernie Starr	
Vieni-Vieni	Rudy Vallee	
Waitin' for the Evening Mail	James Barton	
Was That the Human Thing to Do	Guy Lombardo	
Was There Ever a Pal Like You	Billie Burke	
Wedding of the Painted Doll	Geralding and Anne Beaumont	*Broadway Melody*
What Can I Say After I Say I'm Sorry	Bee Palmer	
When I Grow Too Old to Dream	Harry Richman	*Puttin' on the Ritz*
When the Moon Comes Over the Mountain	Kate Smith	
When the Real Thing Comes Your Way	Buddy Rogers and Nancy Carroll	*Illusion*
When They Cut Down the Old Pine Tree	Rudy Vallee	
When You're Smiling	Rudy Vallee	

Song	Cover Star	Movie
Where the Lazy Daisies Grow	Dan and Schenck	
Who's Sorry Now	Ed Healey and Allen Cross	
Yoo-Hoo	Al Jolson	
You Brought a New Kind of Love to Me	Maurice Chevalier	*The Big Pond*

CHAPTER 9

Shirley Temple and Walt Disney

in Pan Alley's cutoff date has most often been referred to as the early thirties. On April 23, 1928, Shirley Temple, the most famous child star in history was born. Her first movie was produced in 1932. It matters not what period she belongs to. What does matter is her phenomenal talent and appeal. As I listen to a recent release of her early recordings, I am completely overwhelmed by the abundance of charm and entertainment abilities her singing portrays. It is doubtful that her appeal or talent as a child star will ever be equalled.

Lucky Lindy's successful transatlantic flight in 1927 must have influenced Walt Disney to produce the following year, his first animated cartoon, "Plane Crazy." It was the beginning of the Disney dynasty. From Walt Disney's 1933 silly symphony *Three Little Pigs* came the first hit song written for an animated cartoon, "Who's Afraid of the Big Bad Wolf." This was over forty years ago.

Song sheets associated with Walt Disney and Shirley Temple represent the most coveted of those published in the post–Tin Pan Alley era. Increasing interest is also shown to those issued during World War II.

News, political, and exposition songs at any given point in time are always popular with the collector. In addition to these, the post–Tin Pan Alley song covers show an abundance of star celebrities from radio, records, or motion pictures.

Shirley Temple Movies and Songs

1934 *Bright Eyes*
On the Good Ship Lollipop

1934 *Stand Up and Cheer*
On Account of I Love You
Baby, Take a Bow

1935 *Curly Top*
Animal Crackers in my Soup
When I Grow Up

1935 *The Littlest Rebel*
The Little Colonel
Polly-Wolly-Doodle

1936 *Dimples*
He Was a Dandy
Hey, What Did the Bluebird Say
Picture Me Without You

1936 *Captain January*
At the Codfish Ball
Early Bird
The Right Somebody to Love

1936 *Stowaway*
Goodnight My Love
I Want to Go to the Zoo

1936 *Stowaway* (cont'd)
You Gotta S-m-i-l-e to Be H-a-double-p-y
1936 *Poor Little Rich Girl*
But Definitely
Oh! My Goodness
When I'm With You
You've Gotta Eat Your Spinach, Baby
1938 *Little Miss Broadway*
Be Optimistic
How Can I Thank You
If the World Were All Paper

Swing Me an Old Fashioned Song
We Should Be Together
1938 *Just Around The Corner*
I Love to Walk in the Rain
This Is a Happy Little Ditty
1938 *Rebecca of Sunnybrook Farm*
Come and Get Your Happiness
1940 *Young People*
Tra-La-La-La
1940 *The Bluebird*
Lay-De-O

Walt Disney Movies, Their Dates and Songs

1933 *Three Little Pigs*
Who's Afraid of the Big Bad Wolf?
1937 *Snow White and the Seven Dwarfs*
Bluddle-Uddle-Um-Dum
The Dwarf's Yodel Song
Heigh Ho
I'm Wishing
One Song
Some Day My Prince Will Come
Whistle While You Work
1940 *Pinocchio*
Give a Little Whistle
Hi Diddle Dee Dee
I've Got No Strings
Little Woodenhead
When You Wish Upon a Star
1941 *The Reluctant Dragon*
I'm a Reluctant Dragon
Oh Fleecy Cloud
Radish So Red
'Tis Evening
To an Upside Down Cake
1941 *Dumbo*
All Aboard
Baby of Mine
Look Out For Mr. Stark
Pink Elephants on Parade
When I See an Elephant Fly
1942 *Bambi*
Let's Sing a Gay Little Spring Song

1942 *Bambi* (cont'd)
Little April Shower
Love is a Song
The Thumper Song
Twitterpated
1943 *Saludos Amigos*
Brazil
Saludos Amigos
Tico Tico
1945 *The Three Caballeros*
Baia
Mexico
Os Quendius Do Yaya
The Three Caballeros
You Belong To My Heart
1946 *Make Mine Music*
After You've Gone
All the Cats Join In
Blue Bayou
Casey the Pride of Them All
Johnny Fedora and Alice Blue Bonnet
The Martins and the Coys
Two Silhouettes
Without You
1946 *Song of the South*
Everybody's Got a Laughing Place
How Do You Do
Let the Rain Pour Down
Sooner or Later
Sound of the South

1946 *Song of the South* (cont'd)
    That's What Uncle Remus Said
    Who Wants to Live Like That
    You'll Always Be the One I Love
    Zip-A-Dee-Doo-Dah

1947 *Fun and Fancy Free*
    Fee Fi Fo Fum
    Fun and Fancy Free
    I'm a Happy-Go-Lucky Fellow
    Lazy Countryside
    My Favorite Dream
    Say It With a Slap
    Too Good to Be True

1948 *Melody Time*
    Blame It on the Samba
    Blue Shadows on the Trail
    The Flight of the Bumblebee
    Little Toot
    The Lord is Good to Me
    Melody Time
    Once Upon a Wintertime
    Pecos Bill
    The Pioneer Song
    Trees

1948 *So Dear to My Heart*
    County Fair
    It's What You Do With What You Got
    Lavender Blue
    Ol' Dan Patch
    So Dear to My Heart
    Stick-To-It-Ivity

1948 *Cinderella*
    A Dream Is a Wish Your Heart Makes
    Bibbidi-Bobbidi-Boo
    Cinderella
    Sing Sweet Nightingale
    So This Is Love
    The Work Song

1949 *Ichabod and Mr. Toad*
    The Headless Horseman
    Ichabod
    Katrina
    Merrily on Our Way

1951 *Alice in Wonderland*
    A-E-I-O-U
    A Very Merry Unbirthday
    Alice in Wonderland
    All in a Golden Afternoon
    I'm Late
    In a World of My Own
    March of the Cards
    Old Father William
    Painting the Roses Red
    'Twas Brillig
    Very Good Advice
    The Walrus and the Carpenter
    We'll Smoke the Blighter Out

1953 *Peter Pan*
    A Pirate's Life
    The Elegant Captain Hook
    Never Smile at a Crocodile
    Tee-Dum-Tee-Dum
    What Makes the Red Man Red
    You Can Fly, You Can Fly, You Can
      Fly
    Your Mother and Mine

1954 *Twenty Thousand Leagues Under the
    Sea*
    A Whale of a Tale

1955 *Davy Crockett King of the Wild
    Frontier*
    The Ballad of Davy Crockett
    Farewell

1955 *Lady and the Tramp*
    Bella Notte
    He's a Tramp
    La La Lu
    Peace on Earth
    Siamese Cat Song

1956 *The Great Locomotive Chase*
    Sons of Old Aunt Dinah

1956 *Westward Ho the Wagons!*
    I'm Lonely, My Darlin'
    John Colter
    Pioneers Prayer
    Westward Ho the Wagons!

1956 *Westward Ho the Wagons* (cont'd)
Wringle, Wrangle
1956 *Davy Crockett and the River Pirates*
Ballad of Davy Crockett
King of the River
Yaller, Yaller Gold
1957 *Johnny Tremain*
Johnny Tremain
The Liberty Tree
1957 *Perri*
And Now to Sleep
Break of Day
Together Time
1957 *Old Yeller*
Old Yeller
1957 *The Light in the Forest*
I Asked My Love a Favor
The Light in the Forest
1959 *Tonka*
Tonka
1959 *Sleeping Beauty*
Hail the Princess Aurora
I Wonder
Once Upon a Dream
The Skump Song
The Sleeping Beauty Song
1959 *Darby O'Gill and the Little People*
Pretty Irish Girl
The Wishing Song
1959 *Third Man on the Mountain*
Climb the Mountain
Goodnight Valais
1960 *Toby Tyler or Ten Weeks With a Circus*
Biddle-De-Dee
1960 *Ten Who Dared*
Jolly Rovers
Roll Along
Ten Who Dared
1960 *Swiss Family Robinson*
My Heart Is an Island
1960 *The Sign of Zorro*
The Sign of Zorro

1961 *A Hundred and One Dalmatians*
Cruella De Ville
Dalmatian Plantation
Kanine Krunchie Commercial
1961 *The Absent Minded Professor*
Midfield Fight Song
Sweet Betsy of Pike
1961 *The Parent Trap*
For Now, For Always
Let's Get Together
The Parent Trap
1961 *Babes in Toyland*
Castle in Spain
Floretta
The Forest of No Return
I Can't Do the Sum
Just A Toy
Just a Whisper Away
Lemonade
March of the Toys
Slowly He Sank into the Sea
Toyland
We Won't Be Happy Till We Get It
The Workshop Song
1962 *The Moon Pilot*
Seven Moons of Beta Lyrae
True Love's an Apricot
The Void
1962 *Bon Voyage*
Bon Voyage
1962 *Big Red*
Emile's Reel
Mon Amour Perdu
1962 *Legend of Lobo*
Legend of Lobo
1962 *The Search of the Castaways*
The Castaways Theme
Enjoy It
Grimpons
Merci Beaucoup
1963 *Miracle of the White Stallions*
Just Say Auf Wiedersehen

1963 *Savage Sam*
The Land of the Wild Countree
1963 *Summer Magic*
Beautiful Beulah
Femininity
Flitterin'
On the Front Porch
The Pink of Perfection
Summer Magic
The Ugly Bug Ball
1963 *The Sword in the Stone*
A Most Befuddling Thing
Blue Oak Tree
The Legend of the Sword in Stone
Mad Madame Mim
That's What Makes the World Go
Round
1964 *The Misadventures of Merlin Jones*
Merlin Jones
1964 *The Three Lives of Thomasina*
The Three Lives of Thomasina
1964 *The Moon Spinners*
The Moon Spinner Song
1964 *Mary Poppins*
A Man Has Dreams
Chim Chim Cheree
Feed the Birds
Fidelity Fidieciary Bank
I Love to Laugh
Jolly Holiday
Let's Go Fly a Kite
The Life I Lead
The Perfect Nanny
Sister Suffragette
Spoonful of Sugar
Stay Awake
Step in Time
Supercalifragilisticexpialidocious

1965 *Those Calloways*
The Cabin Raising Song
Rhyme Around
1965 *The Monkey's Uncle*
The Monkey's Uncle
1965 *That Darn Cat*
That Darn Cat
1966 *Follow Me Boys*
Follow Me Boys
1967 *Monkeys Go Home*
Joie de Vivre
1967 *The Adventures of Bull Whip Griffin*
California Gold
Girls of San Francisco
Whoever You Are
1967 *The Gnome Mobile*
The Gnome Mobile
1967 *The Jungle Book*
The Bare Necessities
Colonel Hati's March
I Wanna Be Like You
Kaa's Song
My Own Home
That's What Friends Are For
1967 *The Happiest Millionaire*
Are We Dancing?
Bye-Uumpum Pum
Detroit
Fortuosity
I'll Always Be Irish
It Won't Be Long 'Til Christmas
Let's Have a Drink on It
Strengthen the Dwelling
There Are Those
Valentine Candy
Watch Your Footwork
What's Wrong With That?

CHAPTER 10

Recap

Song sheet collecting is full of surprises. For me it happens with regularity, whetting my appetite and spurring me on to further research. An example was the discovery of a double song sheet. It was folded in a Z with two front covers—"She's Wonderful" by Walter Donaldson and Gus Kahn on one side and "You're in Love and I'm in Love" by Walter Donaldson on the other.

On occasion I will pick up a song that seems to have a particularly attractive cover. It turns out to be the reverse of the song sheet.

An unexpected personal gratification came when I found a song sheet entitled "Echoes From the Snowball Club (Ragtime Waltz")" and composed by Harry Guy. It was my pleasure to have spent an afternoon with him in 1946 at his home in Detroit, Michigan. Mr. Guy told me he was responsible for having written the first Ragtime waltz. The song was published in 1898. I believe it to be the one he referred to, since I vaguely recall something about "Snowballs," thinking at the time what an odd name for a song. Harry Guy is mentioned along with other Ragtime luminaries as part of the musical rebellion of the early 1900s.

It has been an exciting trip for me down Tin Pan Alley through the song sheets. It has entailed two years of almost constant research, sorting and resorting hundreds of song sheets, gathering bits and pieces of information. A trek to the public library was a monthly ritual, and I always returned home with an armload of books to study, neglecting family and friends, and knowing I had a dragon by the tail, but enjoying it nonetheless.

You must have come to the conclusion that I have a special preference for Tin Pan Alley era songs. This is true although I do concede to the fact that hundreds of beautifully written songs have been published in the post–Tin Pan Alley era. I also agree that a great deal of garbage spewed out of the Alley during its lifetime, but in the main we were sated with excellence in popular song writing, and these same songs are the Tin Pan Alley classics of today.

Bibliography

Becker, Stephan. *Comic Art in America*. New York: Simon & Schuster, Inc., 1959.

Berger, Kenneth. *The March King and his Band.* Exposition Press, Inc., 1957.

Blesh, Rudi, and Janis, Harriet. *They All Played Ragtime*. Rev. ed. New York: Oak Publications, 1971.

Blum, Daniel. *A Pictorial History of the Silent Screen*. New York: Grosset & Dunlap, Inc., 1972.

Ewen, David. *Complete Book of American Musical History*. New York: Henry Holt and Co., 1958.

Ewen, David. *Great Men of American Popular Song*. Englewood Cliffs, N.J.: Prentice-Hall, Inc., 1970.

Goldberg, Isaac. *Tin Pan Alley*. New York: Frederick Unger Publishing Co., Inc., 1961.

Jones, Le Roi. *Blues People*. New York: William Morrow & Co., Inc., 1963.

Levy, Lester S. *Grace Notes in American History*. Norman, Oklahoma: University of Oklahoma Press, 1967.

Marcuse, Maxwell F. *Tin Pan Alley in Gaslight*. Watkins Glen, N.Y.: Century House, Inc., 1959.

Marks, E. B. *They All Had Glamour*. New York: Julian Messner, 1944.

Marks, E. B. *They All Sang*. New York: The Viking Press, Inc., 1935.

Martin, Deac. *Musical Americana*. Englewood Cliffs, N.J.: Prentice-Hall, Inc., 1972.

Mattfield, Julius. *Variety Music Cavalcade*. Englewood Cliffs, N.J.: Prentice-Hall, Inc., 1952.

Mattin, Leonard. *The Disney Films*. New York: Crown Publishers, Inc., 1973.

McClinton, Katherine. *Art Deco*. New York: Clarkson N. Potter, Inc., 1972.

Panassie, Hughes. *The Real Jazz*. New York: Smith, Durrell, Inc., 1942.

Schickel, Richard. *The Disney Version*. New York: Simon & Schuster, Inc., 1968.

Schuller, Gunther. *Early Jazz*. New York: Oxford University Press, 1968.

Slide, Anthony. *Early American Cinema*. Cranbury, N.J.: A. S. Barnes & Co., Inc., 1970.

Southern, Eileen. *The Music of Black America—a History*. New York: W. W. Norton & Co., Inc., 1971.

Spaeth, Sigmund. *The History of Popular Music in America*. New York: Random House, Inc., 1948.

Witmark, Isadore, and Goldberg, Isaac. *The Story of the House of Witmark*. New York: Lee Furman, Inc., 1939.

Current Values by Category

The song sheet is multifaceted. Any attempt at compiling a price guide for 50,000 to 100,000 songs would be virtually impossible. In addition the individual song sheet must be given the following considerations:

Age	Composers
Popularity	Performers
Scarcity	Identical songs (Different
Cover artists	covers or stars)
Categories	Early or late issue
Condition	

With this in mind, the logical approach would be by category. But even this leaves a great deal to be reckoned with.

To my knowledge there has not been a book published, which has seriously dealt with the vast number of categories (or the pricing thereof) sheet music has to offer. My twelve year involvement in antiques, flea marketing, and sheet music collecting gives me, I hope, the required experience and background necessary to make at least a genuine effort in this direction.

The normally unattractive stack of music in various stages of deterioration encountered at antique shops, flea markets, and secondhand stores, averages in price from 25¢ to $2.50. With this as a cost basis, it would be reasonable to assume that any large (pre–World War I) *mint* condition song sheet would have a minimum value of $3.00. Any standard size (post–World War I to 1940) *mint* condition song sheet should have a minimum value of $2.00. If the same criteria are applied to the small (World War I transitional) song sheet and the short period of time during which it was published is taken into consideration, a minimum of $4.00 is appropriate. Of course, these prices do not apply to music instruction and orchestral arrangements.

Using *mint* condition as the standard to work from, the following gauge should be used in arriving at a realistic value.

Introducing the Song Sheet	Condition	Value
	Mint; near music store condition—absence of written or stamped names, smears, tears, or frays	100%
	Music store stamp; otherwise very good	90%
	Owner's name in ink; otherwise very good	75%
	Carefully trimmed edges; otherwise very good	65%
	Separated cover; otherwise very good	55%
	Dog-eared or slightly frayed	50%
	Torn, somewhat smeared, or badly frayed	25%
	Dirty, badly torn, or incomplete	10%

The prices listed on the following pages are for *mint* condition only.

Hits Without Words and the Blues

The Cake walks
Basic price $8.00 (Only large size issued)

Kerry Mills	$10.00	Harrigan and Braham	$10.00
Ben Harney	$10.00	Monroe Rosenfeld	$10.00
William Krell	$10.00	Scott Joplin	$14.00

Rags

Basic price: $7.00 (Only large size issued)

Scott Joplin	$14.00	Chris Smith	$10.00
His St. Louis World's		Charles Roberts	$ 9.00
Fair song "The		C. Luckyth Roberts	$ 9.00
Cascades"	$15.00	Charles Lamb	$10.00
James Scott	$11.00	George Botsford	$ 9.00
Tom Turpin	$10.00	Eubie Blake	$ 9.00
His St. Louis World's		Hal Nichols	$ 8.00
Fair song "St. Louis		Percy Wenrich	$ 8.00
Rag"	$13.00	Ed Claypoole	$ 8.00

Fox trots
Basic price: $5.00

Chris Smith	$7.50	Joe Jordan	$6.00
Ed Claypoole	$7.00	Will Cooke	$6.00
C. Luckyth Roberts	$6.50		

Hesitations
Basic Price: $5.00

Clarence Jones	$6.00	Lionel Baxter	$5.00
Any of the well-known rag writers	$6.00		

Miscellaneous dances
Basic price: $4.00
Any of the well-known rag writers $6.00

Turkey trot	$7.50	Kangaroo dip	$7.50
Fish walk	$7.50	Texas Tommy	$7.50
The snake	$7.50	Crab step	$7.50
Grizzly bear	$7.50	The Charleston	$7.50

Add $3.00 to the price of any of these song sheets with a picture of Irene and Vernon Castle or Maurice Mouret and Florence Walton.

Indian intermezzos and ballads
Basic price: Large $5.00   Standard $3.00

Kerry Mills	$7.50	Charles Johnson	$6.50
Neil Moret	$7.50	Percy Wenrich	$6.00

Marches
Basic price: Large $3.00   Standard $2.00

John P. Sousa	$12.00	Charles Johnson	$6.00
George Rosey	$ 5.00	Abe Holzmann	$4.00
Paul Lincke	$ 4.00	Harry J. Lincoln	$4.00
For E. T. Paull see Chapter 6.			

The Blues
Basic price: Large $8.00   Standard $5.00

W. C. Handy's large size $12.00. His "Memphis Blues" published by Theron C. Bennett, the first blues published, are valued at $25.00. His own published version of "Memphis Blues" would have an increased value. If you can find it, it's worth $40.00. The Joe Morris publication that was transferred from Theron C. Bennett would be priced the same as any large size W. C. Handy Blues.

Miscellaneous Categories

The Tear-jerkers
Basic price: $6.00 (Only large size issued)

Paul Dresser	$8.00	Charles K. Harris	$ 7.00
Harry Kennedy	$7.00	After the Ball	$10.00
Gussie L. Davis	$9.00	Ed Marks and Joe Stern	$ 7.00

Alcohol and prohibition
Basic price: Large $10.00   Standard $5.00

Food and nonalcoholic beverages
Basic price: Large $8.50   Standard $6.00

Wearing apparel
Basic price: Large $9.00 (Big hats, peg trousers, outstanding) Standard $5.50

Locations
Large size only

Broadway	$7.50	Cities	$6.50
Dixie	$5.00	States	$6.00
Ireland	$3.50	Hawaii	$3.50
Rivers	$3.00	Others (Countries, etc.)	$4.00

Coon songs
Basic price: Large $6.50   Standard $4.00

Kerry Mills	$8.50	Ben Harney	$8.00
Charles Johnson	$7.00	Harry Von Tilzer	$7.00

Mother
Basic price: Large $5.00   Standard $3.00   Before 1890 $9.00

Girl's names and portraits
Names

Rose	$5.00	Others	$4.00

Portraits

Girl's portraits on standard sized song sheets, because of their appeal are on an equal basis with the large song sheets.

Big Hats	$6.00	Manning	$5.00
Others	$4.00		

Transportation and communication
Large

Automobile	$13.00	Railroad	$ 8.00
Steamboat	$ 7.00	Telegraph	$11.00
Telephone	$ 8.00	U. S. Mail	$10.00
Airplane	$11.00	Balloon	$11.00
Bicycle	$10.00	Dirigible	$11.00
Walking	$ 4.50	Glider	$11.00
Trolley	$10.00		

Standard

Automobile	$ 7.50	Railroad	$ 5.00
Steamboat	$ 4.50	Telegraph	$ 5.50
Telephone	$ 5.00	U. S. Mail	$ 5.00
Airplane	$ 6.00	Balloon	$ 6.00
Lindberg	$10.00	Dirigible	$ 6.00
Bicycle	$ 5.00	Glider	$ 6.00
Walking	$ 3.50	Trolley	$ 5.00

Current events, political, exposition, dedications
Large

Presidents	$10.00	Other Politicians	$8.00
Catastrophes	$12.00	Expositions	$9.00
News events	$10.00	Dedications	$6.00

Standard

Presidents	$ 8.00	Other Politicians	$6.00
Catastrophes	$ 9.00	Expositions	$7.00
News events	$ 7.50	Dedications	$4.00

Children

The Children's songs of the Tear-jerker, Mammy croons, and School type were normally large size song sheets. Consequently no standard song sheet price is listed except a general overall price.

Large

Tear-jerker	$7.00	Mammy croons	$9.00
School Days	$6.00	Others	$5.00

Standard

General	$4.00

Flora, Fauna, and other Earth creatures
Large

Flora	$4.00	Fauna	$6.00
Linen	$5.00	Other Earth creatures	$4.50
Roses	$5.00		

Standard

Flora	$3.00	Fauna	$3.50
Linen	$4.00	Other Earth creatures	$4.00
Roses	$4.00		

Novelty Songs

Novelty songs of the twenties and thirties by virtue of their overall cover appeal should have value equal to the large size song sheets.

Basic price: Large or Standard $6.00

Sports and Games
Large

Sports			
General	$ 7.00	Games	$8.00
Baseball	$10.00		

Standard

Sports			
General	$ 5.00	Games	$6.50
Baseball	$ 6.50		

Conflicts

Spanish-American War	$7.00
World War I	
Large	$7.50
Standard	$6.50
Small	$6.50
Miniature	$9.00

For Norman Rockwell World War I song sheets see "special covers" for pricing.

The Cover Artists

There are exceptional covers by all artists. However, they produced some rather bad ones too. The prices quoted are for their average covers. For Art Deco covers, especially Wohlman and Millard, consult Chapter 7 for pricing.

Large

Starmer	$4.00	Barbelle	$4.50
DeTakacs	$5.50	Pfeiffer	$3.00
Frew	$3.00	Gene Buck	$3.00
R. S.	$4.00		

Standard

Manning	$5.00	Wohlman	$4.00
Millard	$4.00	J. V. R.	$4.00
Barbelle	$4.00	R. S.	$4.00
Perret	$3.50	Politzer	$4.00
Pel Studios	$3.50	Pud Lane	$4.00

Special Covers

E. T. Paull Lithographs
Basic price: Large $12.00   Standard $5.00

Art Deco

Because the twenties and thirties are more truly representative of Art Deco, the standard size song sheets tend to have greater value. C. Luckyth Roberts' "Pork and Beans" (cover artist—deTakacs) appears to be the only song sheet done in *cubism*. This places it in the scarce category with a price of $25.00. All Art Deco in standard size with the exception of Wohlman and Millard are priced at $7.00. Wohlman and Millard are valued at $8.00; large size song sheets at $6.50.

The cartoonists and illustrators

Norman Rockwell		Geo McManus (Bringing Up Father)	$10.00
Large	$22.00		
Small	$14.00	Clare Victor Dwiggins (Ophelia)	$11.50
Hamilton King	$10.00	Harold Gray (Orphan Annie)	$ 9.00
James Montgomery Flagg	$ 8.00	Gaar Williams	$ 7.00
Archie Gunn	$10.00	Paul Fung (Dumb Dora)	$ 5.00
De Beck (Barney Google)	$10.00		

The Linens

Large

Carrie Jacobs-Bond	$6.50	Others	$5.00

Standard

General	$4.00	Carrie Jacobs-Bond	$5.00

Sunday supplements
(Large size with a few exceptions)

General	$2.00	Opper (Happy Hooligan)	$7.50
Cartoonists	$5.00 to $7.50	Swinnerton (Tumble Tom)	$7.00
Shows or stars	$3.00		

Advertising

Wait for the Wagon (Studebaker Company)	$50.00	Song of the Great Big Baked Potato (Northern Pacific Railroad)	$12.00
The Merry Singer (Singer Mfg Company)	$25.00	Way Down Upon The Swanee River (Southern Railroad System)	$ 6.00
Garland Stove Company	$ 5.00	Honeymoon For Three (Chevrolet)	$ 7.00
Bromo Seltzer (colored)	$ 4.00	Milena Two Step (Huntington Piano Company)	$ 6.00
(black and white)	$ 3.00		
Cable March and Two Step (Cable Piano Company)	$ 7.00		

Action Western
Basic price: $6.50 (Only large size issued)

The Entertainment Field

Musical shows
Basic price: $4.00 to $7.50
  Ziegfeld Follies $6.00

Musical Stars (Coonshouters and others)
Basic price: $4.00 to $6.00

Stars listed $7.50 to $10.00

Nora Bayes	Al Jolson
Fannie Bryce	Dick Jose
Emma Carus	Eddie Leonard
George M. Cohan	George Primrose
Barney Fagan	Pat Rooney
Weber and Fields	Lillian Russell
Eddie Foy	Eva Tanguay
Lottie Gilson	Sophie Tucker
Anna Held	Billie West
May Irwin	Bert Williams

The silents
Basic price: General $7.00   Designated theme songs $8.50

Stars listed $8.00

Wallace Beery	
Francis X. Bushman	Mae Marsh
Ruth Chatterton	Nazimova
Jackie Coogan	Pola Negri
Arthur Guy Empey	Mabel Normand
Vera Gordon	Gilbert Roland
Alice Joyce	Gloria Swanson
Harold Lloyd	Pearl White

Stars of radio, record, and talkies

Charlie Chaplin	$15.00
Amos and Andy	$9.00
The following Stars $7.00	
Vilma Bankey	Ted Lewis
Eddie Cantor	Carole Lombard
Helen Kane	Sophie Tucker
Al Jolson	Gloria Swanson

150

The following Stars $5.00

June Caprice   Dick Powell
Bing Crosby   Harry Richman
Gus Edwards   Kate Smith
Ruth Etting   Rudy Vallee

Shirley Temple and Walt Disney

Shirley Temple $7.50   Walt Disney $6.50

Song Sheet Record

Title and composer	Size	Date Purchased	Price Paid

Song Sheet Record

Title and composer	Size	Date Purchased	Price Paid

Song Sheet Record

Title and composer	Size	Date Purchased	Price Paid

Song Sheet Record

Title and composer	Size	Date Purchased	Price Paid

Song Sheet Record

Title and composer	Size	Date Purchased	Price Paid

Song Sheet Record

Title and composer	Size	Date Purchased	Price Paid

Acknowledgements (continued from page 4)
Used by permission of Chappell, Inc.: "The Perfect Song," "One-A-Strike."

Used by permission of Edward B. Marks Music Corp.: "Sweetie Dear," "Pork and Beans," "Tom Tom Tango," "There's No More Buster Brown," "By Heck," "The Bird on Nellie's Hat," "Roll Them Cotton Bales," "Break the News to Mother," "Sob Sister Sadie," "Montmartre Rose," "Hobomoko."

Used by permission of Will Rossiter, 173 W. Madison St., Chicago, Ill. 60602: "Pretzel Pete," "If I Only had a Home Sweet Home."

Used by permission of Walter Kane & Co. Inc.: "Poor Pauline," "One Wonderful Night," "Old Fashioned Roses," "Daddy Long Legs," "In the Evening By the Moonlight in Dear Old Tennessee," "The Flight of the Airship," "When the Bonnie, Bonnie Heather Is Blooming, I'll Return Annie Laurie, to You."

Used by permission of Belwin-Mills Music Publishing Corp.: "I've Gone Goofy Over Miniature Golf," "Love Is Just a Flower," "How 'Ya Gonna Keep 'em Down on the Farm," "As Long as the Shamrocks Grow Green."

Courtesy of the publisher and copyright owner, Shawnee Press, Inc., Delaware Water Gap, PA. 18327: "Red Wing," "The Midnight Fire Alarm," "Paul Revere's Ride."

Used by permission of T. B. Harms Co.: "It's a Hundred to One You're in Love," "Keep Your Foot on the Soft Pedal," "Just Across the Bridge of Gold," "On the New York, New Haven, and Hartford," "Show Me the Way to Go Home," "Weegee, Weegee," "There's a Wireless Station Down in My Heart."

Used by permission of Warner Brothers' Music: "Just a Moment" © 1914 Jerome H. Remick; "The Kangaroo Hop" © 1915 Jerome H. Remick & Co.; "Blame It on the Blues" © 1914 Jerome H. Remick; "He Got Right up on the Wagon" © 1910 Jerome H. Remick; "Macaroni Joe" © 1910 Je-

Acknowledgements

rome H. Remick; "The Rah-Rah Boy" © 1908 Jerome H. Remick & Co.; "I'm on My Way to Reno" © 1910 Jerome H. Remick & Co.; "Back, Back, Back to Baltimore" © 1904 Shapiro, Remick Co.; "Don't Bring Lulu" © 1925 Jerome H. Remick & Co.; "On the 5:15" © 1914 Jerome H. Remick & Co.; 'Tiddle-De-Winks" © 1916 Jerome H. Remick & Co.; "Beautiful Annabel Lee" © 1920 Jerome H. Remick & Co.; "Somebody's Wrong Song" © 1923 Jerome H. Remick & Co.; "Oh You Beautiful Doll" © 1911 Jerome H. Remick & Co.; "Mammy Jinnie's Hall of Fame" © 1917 Jerome H. Remick & Co.; "Heartsease" © 1919 Jerome H. Remick & Co.; "The Murray Walk" © 1914 Jerome H. Remick & Co.; "That Wonderful Mother of Mine" © 1918 Jerome H. Remick & Co.; "Mandalay" © 1924 Jerome H. Remick & Co.; "Baby Sister Blues" © 1926 Jerome H. Remick & Co.; "Just Like a Butterfly" © 1927 Jerome H. Remick & Co.; "Under a Summertime Moon" © 1910 Jerome H. Remick & Co.; "The Glory of Jamestown" © 1907 M. Witmark & Sons; "They Gotta Quit Kickin' My Dawg Around" © 1912 M. Witmark & Sons; "Mister Moving Picture Man" © 1912 Jerome H. Remick & Co.; "The Mocking Birds Are Singing in the Wildwood" © 1906 Jerome H. Remick & Co.; "They Made It Twice as Nice as Paradise and They Called It Dixieland" © 1916 Jerome H. Remick & Co.; "Sweet Patootie Sal" © 1919 Jerome H. Remick & Co.; "The Cup Hunter's March" © 1915 Jerome H. Remick & Co.; "The Road Is Open, Again" © 1933 Jerome H. Remick & Co.; "She's a Mean Job" © 1921 Jerome H. Remick & Co.; "La Veeda" © 1920 Jerome H. Remick & Co.; "So I Took the $5,000" © 1923 Jerome H. Remick & Co.; "Got No Time" © 1925 Jerome H. Remick & Co.; "The Sacred Flame" © 1929 Jerome H. Remick & Co.; "Swanee Butterfly" © 1925 Jerome H. Remick & Co.; "I'm Going to Follow the Boys" © 1917 Jerome H. Remick & Co.; "Bumble Bee" © 1911 Jerome H. Remick & Co.; "Waltz Irresistable" © 1916 Jerome H. Remick & Co.

In addition, song sheet covers used in this book not mentioned here, all rights are reserved to owners of copyrights.

The Walt Disney song sheet listing used is taken from *The Disney Films* by Leonard Maltin © 1973 and used by permission of Crown Publishing Co.

8 7 6 5 4 3 2 1 81 80 79 78 77 76